Endpapers:
Communist Party Secretary General Mikhail Gorbachov being greeted by factory workers.

The photographs contained in this book have been supplied through the courtesy of Novosti Press Agency (APN) and Tass, via their Moscow offices. The editor wishes to espress his thanks for the hospitality and courtesy extended him during his visit to their offices and the speed and efficiency with which they supplied the dated material. Novosti, for example, supplied color photographs plus an English translation of Gorbachov's Chernobyl speech, within a few hours of its television delivery.

GORBACHOV

Михаил Сергеевич ГОРБАЧЕВ

An Understanding of the Soviet Union through his Speeches with Special Reference to his New Rules of the Communist Party.

Edited by Dr. Herbert R. Axelrod
with Lisa Gutschmit

Distributed in the UNITED STATES by T.F.H. Publications, Inc., 211 West Sylvania Avenue, Neptune City, NJ 07753; in CANADA by H & L Pet Supplies Inc., 27 Kingston Crescent, Kitchener, Ontario N2B 2T6; Rolf C. Hagen Ltd., 3225 Sartelon Street, Montreal 382 Quebec; in ENGLAND by T.F.H. Publications Limited, 4 Kier Park, Ascot, Berkshire SL5 7DS; in AUSTRALIA AND THE SOUTH PACIFIC by T.F.H. (Australia) Pty. Ltd., Box 149, Brookvale 2100 N.S.W., Australia; in NEW ZEALAND by Ross Haines & Son, Ltd., 18 Monmouth Street, Grey Lynn, Auckland 2 New Zealand; in SINGAPORE AND MALAYSIA by MPH Distributors (S) Pte., Ltd., 601 Sims Drive, #03/07/21, Singapore 1438; in the PHILIPPINES by Bio-Research, 5 Lippay Street, San Lorenzo Village, Makati Rizal; in SOUTH AFRICA by Multipet Pty. Ltd., 30 Turners Avenue, Durban 4001. Published by T.F.H. Publications, Inc. Manufactured in the United States of America by T.F.H. Publications, Inc.

Contents

Preface 9
Background 21
1. Address by Mikhail Gorbachov at the Opening of the 27th CPSU Congress 29
2. Report by Mikhail Gorbachov to the 27th CPSU Congress 33
3. Speech by Mikhail Gorbachov at the Closing of the 27th CPSU Congress 107
4. Resolution of the 27th CPSU Congress 113
5. Mikhail Gorbachov's Message to the Conference on Disarmament 123
6. Rules of the Communist Party 125
7. Geneva–The United States-Soviet Summit, November 1985 143
TV Address by Mikhail Gorbachov on the Chernobyl Disaster 149
To Visitors of Soviet Pavilion at Expo-86 World Exhibition in Vancouver 188

Dr. Axelrod with Dmitri Tsiganov, first violinist in the Beethoven String Quartet and professor at the Moscow Conservatory, in front of Dmitri Shostakovich's home.

Preface

By Dr. Herbert R. Axelrod

I am neither an expert on Communism nor a Soviet specialist. I have made several dozen trips to the Soviet Union conducting business with the Soviets in the fields of publishing and entertainment. My company has issued hundreds of classical music records produced by the firm Melodiya, the Soviet Union's huge classical music recording studio; video cassettes featuring Soviet opera and ballet; books dealing primarily with music and Soviet musicians. We were able to represent the first Soviet artists to come to America after the signing of the Cultural Exchange Agreement when, in January, 1986 Nikolai Petrov, the pianist, and conductor Yuri Temirkhanov appeared with the New York Philharmonic Orchestra in New York City.

During hundreds of hours of meetings with Soviet musicians like David Oistrakh, Leonid Kogan, Rodion Shchedrin, Tikhon Khrennikov, and most of the upper echelon of performers; during visits to dozens of Soviet homes of both official Party members (including high-

President Reagan and General Secretary Gorbachov in conversation accompanied by smiles during the 1985 summit meeting in Geneva.

Dr. Herbert R. Axelrod with eminent Soviet composers Tikhon Khrennikov (left) and Rodion Shchedrin, in Moscow.

ranking politicians) and low-ranking tropical fish fanciers (I have written dozens of books on the subject), I have developed a certain point of view.

I am, at the present time, preparing a series of books on the Bolshoi Ballet. While many consider the Bolshoi as the world's finest ballet company, it is also the crown jewel of the Soviet cultural-political arena, and the Soviets are justly proud of it. This has brought me into contact with Yuri Grigorovich, the ballet master, and dozens of ballet stars including the incomparable Plisetskaya and Besmertnova.

Add to this background the fact that my father was born in the Russia of 1901 and that my grandfather and his brother were active in the formation of the Russian Communist movement in the late 1800's, and you have the basis for my interest in preparing this book. Uncle Pavel Axelrod, my grandfather's brother, was, they tell me, a forming member of the Communist Party before Lenin. His ideas didn't conform to Lenin's, and he was soon expelled from the Party.

Lest the reader get the wrong idea about me, let it be clear that I am a capitalist and have been very successful in business matters. The objective of this book is not to convert anyone to Communism but rather to present the unadulterated modern Soviet points of view. While both American and Soviet newspapers and magazines are full of highly biased reports of each other's activities, neither side has easy access to raw facts. I hope to present some of the political bases upon which Soviet thought and comment are based . . . these bases are the foundation upon which Mr. Gorbachov's Soviet Union operates.

The truly basic differences between the Soviet and American peoples lie in the histories of the two countries during the past seventy years. Two great, devastating wars were fought on Russian soil with millions of Russians killed and the country all but burned down by the Soviet "scorched earth" policy (Russian troops burned everything of use to the Germans as they retreated to Moscow and Leningrad.) America, on the other hand, while similarly engaged in two World Wars, was spared fighting on its mainland.

As the Russians have experienced such extreme devas-

Yuri Grigorovich, ballet master at Moscow's Bolshoi Ballet.

M. Gorbachov talks to worker I. Prokofiev during his visit to Leningrad.

The official departure ceremony for Indian Prime Minister Ghandi at the Kremlin, May 23, 1985.

tation, they are bound to be suspicious of the actions of any country large enough, or powerful enough, to start another war with them. After all, many Russians told me, "how can America be trusted if their two worst enemies during World War II (Germany and Japan) are now their best friends, and their ally during World War II (meaning the Soviet Union) is now considered their most serious enemy.?"

The Russians also bring up another set of political observations that the ordinary Soviet citizen seeks to have "friendly Americans" answer. "How can you Americans call yourselves a peace-loving, moderate, tolerant people, when you are the only country in the world to ever use an atomic bomb? Your war with Japan had almost reached the Japanese mainland and it was only a matter of days before they collapsed. President Truman justified this action by arguing that he didn't care how many Japanese he killed as long as his act saved one American life." This logic is very frightening to the common Soviet citizen and there isn't much to be said to convince them differently. They are firm believers in taking lessons from history.

The next fact the Soviets love to discuss is: "Let's look at the history of the world since the end of the Second World War. Let's count the number of countries which have changed their governments. How many have chosen the kind of democracy preached and practiced by America? Not many. Perhaps only a few very small nations like Israel . . . and Israel continues experimenting with Socialist concepts and their kibbutzim is strictly modelled after Communist theories. Socialism, Marxism and Communism have been adapted in varying degrees by more people in the world, during the last 40 years, than all the American-style democracies since the beginning of time?"

One other point is often raised by my Soviet contacts. "How can we ever trust America? They turn their back on their best friends, and look what happens. The Shah of Iran was a close ally; they not only helped kick him out of power, but they didn't even want to let him be treated for cancer in America and forced into a search for a safe place to die! The same is true of Haiti's Duva-

Dr. Herbert Axelrod with world famous ballerina Maya Plisetskaya.

lier and the Philippines' Marcos. It has been shown historically that it pays to be at odds with America. They have been much kinder to China, a Communist state, than they are to almost all the countries in South America. They even sell us wheat cheaper than they sell it to their allies. We Russians don't really understand this."

The whole world wants a "just, lasting peace." How that will be achieved is the basis for modern Soviet-American relations. At the time of this writing neither side trusts the other, perhaps with good reason. But one thing leads me to cautious optimism: I have never met a Soviet citizen who didn't express an admiration for American people in one way or another; and I never met an American who wasn't happy to meet any of my Soviet guests and who didn't remark about "how civilized they are!"

I am firmly convinced that peace will come between the USA and the USSR. But it will be built slowly . . . man by man . . and only with such programs as the Soviet-American Cultural Exchange and the Soviet-American Friendship organizations. Any alternative conclusion would lead me to think of the extinction of the planet Earth which, when you think about it, is a very hostile planet.

The Gorbachovs visiting a Pioneer camp.

Gorbachov being inducted as an honorary member of the Pioneers.

Gorbachov during an inspection tour of a machinery factory.

The Party General Secretary discusses items of manufacture with a worker at the Togliatti automobile factory.

New Soviet Leader Gorbachov views the funeral bier of Konstantin Chernenko on March 12, 1985.

Background

Mikhail Sergeyevich Gorbachov was born on March 2, 1931 in the village of Privolnoye in the Stavropol region of Southern Russia, north of the Caucasus.

The son of peasants, he worked at a machine-tractor station in the grain-growing area near his home.

In 1952, he entered the prestigious Moscow State University. There he joined the Communist Party and became a Communist Youth League Organizer. After graduating with a law degree in 1955, he decided to pursue a career as a Party professional. He returned to Stavropol, where he specialized in running collective farms and enjoyed a steady rise within the Party until 1970, when at the age of 39 he was named First Secretary of the regional Party organization. This post brought him into the Central Committee.

In 1978, Gorbachov came to Moscow as the Central Committee's Secretary for Agriculture. In 1980, the death of Party Secretary Fyodor Kulakov created an opening, and Gorbachov was named a full member to Brezhnev's Politburo at the remarkably young age of 49. Facilitating his rapid advance through the ranks of the Party were two powerful mentors, both of whom were born in Stavropol: Mikhail Suslov, leading party ideologist, and Yuri Andropov, then head of the KGB.

Under Andropov, Gorbachov continued to control the country's agricultural programs and was also given key responsibilities in foreign affairs, economics, and party cadres.

As Andropov's health declined, he relied increasingly on Gorbachov as his closest lieutenant. It was Gorbachov who oversaw changes in the Party ranks and experiments in industrial management and who shuttled between the hospital and the Kremlin carrying Andropov's orders to the Politburo.

When Andropov died, there was speculation that Gorbachov would succeed him. A Politburo comprised of aging Brezhnev appointees, however, apparently felt that it was too early to give power to the new

Mikhail Gorbachov attends festivities at a Crimean Pioneer Camp. Seated with him are his wife, granddaughter and daughter.

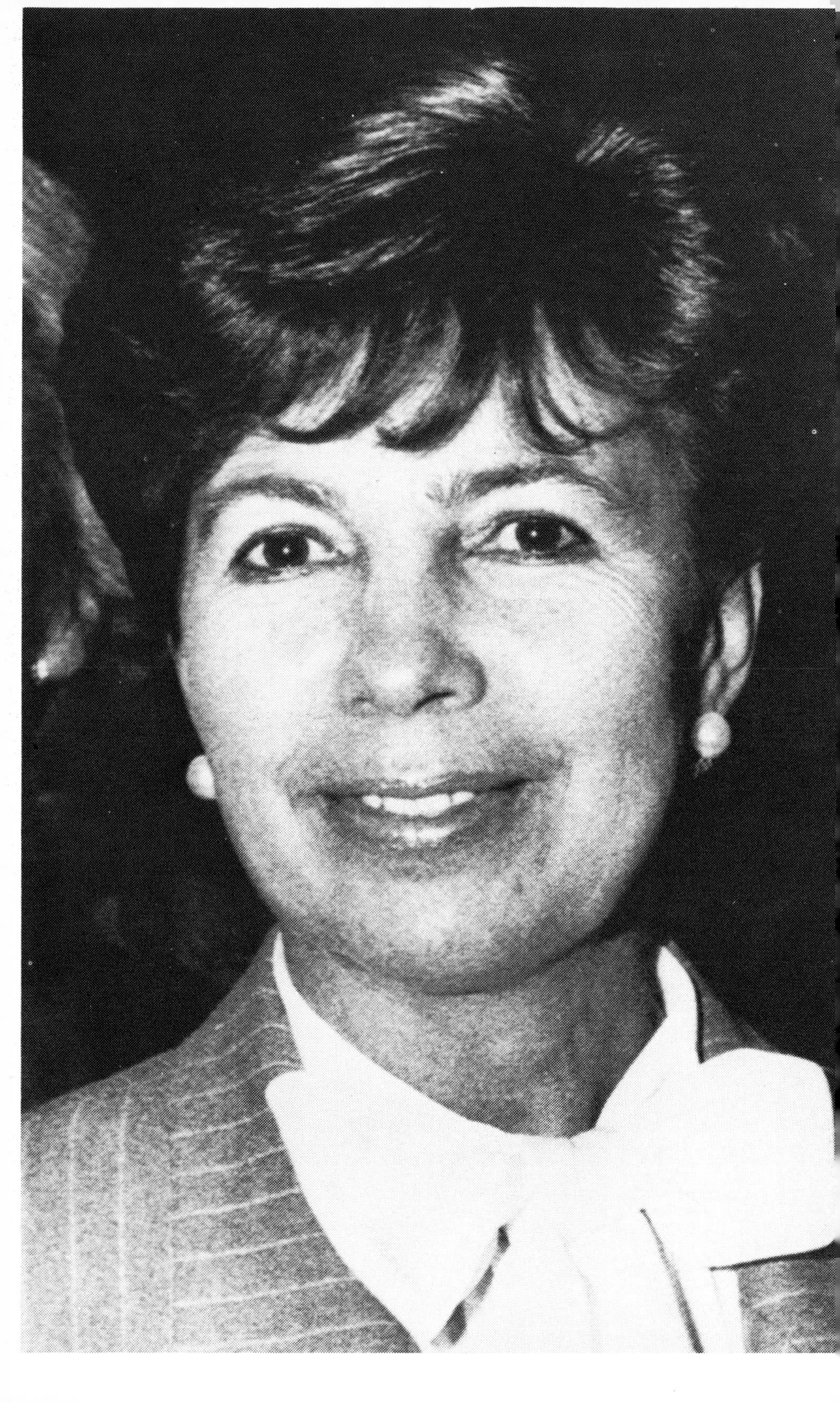

General Secretary talking to residents of the Kuibishev region in April 1986

generation of leaders. Under Chernenko, Gorbachov was, officially, Party Secretary for Ideology and, unofficially, the heir apparent.

On March 11, only four hours after the announcement of Chernenko's death, the Communist Party Central Committee unanimously elected Gorbachov as the Party General Secretary. At 54, he was the youngest member of the Politburo and the youngest Soviet leader in six decades. The first Soviet leader born after the 1917 Bolshevik revolution, and too young to have fought in the Second World War, Gorbachov represented a change from the Old to the New Guard. His image is very different from that of his predecessors. His appearance as a "man of the 1980's" is enhanced by his wife's stylishness and visibility and by his own ability to project simultaneously charisma, affability, and unmistakable resolve.

Raisa Gorbachov is a very culturally inclined worldy woman, and it is fair to assume she will greatly influence Minister of Culture Vasily G. Zakharov.

While in Paris on his official visit in 1985 Gorbachov visited Lenin's apartment (now a museum).

Gorbachov visiting an airplane factory in Kiev in July, 1985.

A worker at the Kuibishev candy factory being greeted by M. Gorbachov.

The U.S. Secretary of State chatting with Soviet Leader Gorbachov before they started talks in the Kremlin on November 5, 1985.

1

Address by Mikhail Gorbachov at the Opening of the 27th CPSU Congress

On behalf of the Party's Central Committee I greet the foreign guests of the 27th Congress of the Communist Party of the Soviet Union assembled here. Taking part in its proceedings, you could see how great the significance of the Congress is in the life of our Party, in the life of the people.

The Congress laid down the general line of the CPSU for an exceptionally responsible and, in effect, crucial stage of the country's development—a line towards accelerating the socio-economic development and consolidating peace on Earth. Its implementation will take Soviet society to a qualitatively new level, and the advantages of socialism in the economy, science and culture, democracy and in the people's entire way of life will be fully disclosed.

You have had an opportunity to feel the atmosphere of the Congress—exacting, creative and businesslike in line with the Party's spirit. The envoys of the Party, representing all strata of Soviet society, all nations and ethnic groups of our Motherland, were unanimous in their principled assessments of the tasks confronting us, and expressed the will and determination to carry them into effect.

I want to stress: no matter what domestic or foreign policy issues the Leninist Party should tackle, it has always considered itself an integral part of all the revolutionary, democratic and progressive forces. We take stock of the fact that every one of our successes, every victory in the struggle for the goals and ideals of the October Revolution, strengthen the potential of peace and social progress. In this, as the Congress emphasized, the CPSU sees its main international duty, and it will fulfil it to the end.

A key place at the Congress was held by the problems of war and peace, and the elimination of the nuclear threat. Nuclear catastrophe must be prevented. It is necessary and possible to build a world without threats, a world of good-neighbourliness, a world in which every nation would hold a worthy place respected by others. The Soviet Union would like to see precisely such a world and wants to be a part of it. And the Congress has confirmed this.

Dear Comrades and Friends, you have been not only guests at our Congress but, as we believe, also its participants. And you have made your contribution to its work.

You did this by supporting the spirit of renewal which prevailed in the hall of the Kremlin Palace, and the foreign policy strategy of the CPSU.

By sharing with the delegates to the Congress your views, assessments and ideas, your own vision of our multiform, contradictory but, on the whole, integral world.

By, at last, finding the time and desire for meetings and talks with Soviet people—Communists and non-Party people alike. And such meetings offer a splendid opportunity for coming to know and understand each other better, for displaying our common internationalist feelings. Those were really cordial, unforgettable meetings.

Gorbachov speaking to the workers of the city of Togliatti.

ЗДА КПСС – В ЖИЗНЬ !

2

Report by Mikhail Gorbachov to the 27th CPSU Congress

Here follows the full text of the political report of the CPSU Central Committee to the 27th Congress of the Communist Party of the Soviet Union delivered by Comrade Mikhail Gorbachov, the General Secretary of the CPSU Central Committee, on February 25, 1986:

The 27th Congress of the CPSU has gathered at an abrupt turning point in the life of the country and the contemporary world as a whole. We are beginning our work with a deep understanding of our responsibility to the Party and the Soviet people. It is our task to conceptualise broadly, in Lenin's style, the times we are living in, and to work out a realistic, thoroughly weighed programme of action that will organically blend the grandeur of our aims with the realism of our capabilities, and the Party's plans with the hopes and aspirations of every person. The resolutions of the 27th Congress will determine both the character and the rate of our movement towards a qualitatively new condition of the Soviet socialist society for years and decades ahead.

The Congress is to discuss and adopt a new edition of the Programme of the CPSU, amendments to the Party Rules, and Guidelines for economic development in the next five years and the longer term. I need hardly mention what enormous importance these documents have for our Party, our state, and our people. Not only do they contain an assessment of the past and a definition of the urgent tasks, but also a glimpse into the future. They speak of what the Soviet Union will be like as it enters the 21st century, of the image of socialism and its positions in the international arena, of the future of humanity.

Soviet society has gone a long way in its development since the now operative Party Programme was adopted. In substance, we have built the whole country anew, have made tremendous headway in the economic, cultural, and social fields, and have raised generations of builders of the new society. We have blazed the trail into outer space for humanity. We have secured strategic military parity and have thereby substantially restricted imperialism's aggressive plans and capabilities to start a nuclear war. The positions of our motherland and of world socialism in the international arena have grown considerably stronger.

The path travelled by the country, its economic, social and cultural achievements, convincingly confirm the validity of the Marxist-Leninist doctrine, and socialism's tremendous potential as embodied in the progress of Soviet society. We can be legitimately proud of everything that has been achieved in these years of intense labour and struggle.

While duly commending the achievements, the leadership of the CPSU considers it to be its duty to tell the Party and the people honestly and frankly about the deficiencies in our political and practical activities, the unfavourable tendencies in the economy and the social and moral sphere, and about the reasons for them. For a number of years the deeds and actions of Party and government bodies tailed behind the needs of the times and life—not only because of objective factors, but also for reasons above all of a subjective order. The problems in the country's development built up more rapidly than they were being solved. The inertness and stiffness of the

Mikhail Gorbachov, during an official trip to the United Kingdom in January 1985, before Konstantin Chernenko's death.

forms and methods of administration, the decline of dynamism in our work, and an escalation of bureaucracy—all this was doing no small damage. Signs of stagnation had begun to surface in the life of society.

The situation called for change, but a peculiar psychology—how to improve things without changing anything—took the upper hand in the central bodies and, for that matter, at local level as well. But that cannot be done, comrades. Stop for an instant, as they say, and you fall behind a mile. We must not evade the problems that have arisen. That sort of attitude is much too costly to the country, the state and the Party. So let us say it loud and clear!

The priority task is to overcome the negative factors in society's socio-economic development as rapidly as possible, to impart to it the essential dynamism and acceleration, to draw to the maximum on the lessons of the past, so that the decisions we adopt for the future should be explicitly clear and considered, and the concrete actions purposeful and effective.

The situation has come to a turning point not only in internal but also in external affairs. The changes in current world affairs are so deep-going and significant that they require reassessment and comprehensive analysis of all factors. The situation created by the nuclear confrontation calls for new approaches, methods, and forms of relations between the different social systems, states and regions.

The arms race started by imperialism has resulted in that the 20th century in world politics is ending with the question of whether humanity manages to elude the nuclear danger or the policy of confrontation will take precedence, increasing the probability of nuclear conflict. The capitalist world has not abandoned the ideology and policy of hegemonism, its rulers have not yet lost the hope of taking social revenge, and continue to indulge themselves with illusions of superior strength. The sober view of what is going on is hewing its way forward with great difficulty through a dense thicket of prejudices and preconceptions in the thinking of the ruling class. But the complexity and acuteness of this moment in history makes it increasingly vital to outlaw nuclear weapons, destroy them and other weapons of mass annihilation completely, and improve international relations.

The fact that the Party has deeply understood the fundamentally new situation inside the country and in the world arena, and that it appreciates its responsibility for the country's future, and has the will and resolve to carry out the requisite change, is borne out by the adoption at the April 1985 plenary meeting of the decision to accelerate the socio-economic development of our society.

Formulating the long-term and fundamental tasks, the Central Committee has consistently taken guidance in Marxism-Leninism, the truly scientific theory of social development. It expresses the vital interests of the working people, and the ideals of social justice. It derives its vitality from its everlasting youthfulness, its constant capacity for development and creative generalisation of the new facts and phenomena, and from its experience of revolutionary struggle and social reconstruction.

Any attempts at turning the theory by which we are guided into an assortment of ossified schemes and prescriptions valid everywhere and in all contingencies is most definitely contrary to the essence and spirit of Marxism-Leninism. Lenin wrote back in 1917 that Marx and Engels had rightly ridiculed the "mere memorising and repetition of 'formulas', that at best are capable only of marking out *general* tasks, which are necessarily modifiable by the *concrete* economic and political conditions of each particular *period* of the historical process." *(Collected Works,* Vol. 24, p. 43.) Those are the words, comrades, that everyone of us must ponder and act upon.

The concrete economic and political situation we are in, and the particular period of the historical process that Soviet society and the whole world are going through, require that the Party and its every member display their creativity, their capacity for innovation and skill to transcend the framework of habitual but already outdated notions.

A far-flung, outspoken and constructive examination of all the crucial problems of our life and of Party policy has taken place during the discussion of the pre-Congress documents. We have come to the Congress enriched by the wisdom and experience of the whole Party, the whole people.

We can now see more clearly what has to be done and in what order, and what levers we must set in motion for our progress to acquire the desired acceleration.

Gorbachov receiving the President of the People's Republic of Mozambique in April, 1986.

Gorbachov attending the exhibition "The Intensification-90" in May, 1985.

These days, many things, in fact everything, will depend on how effectively we succeed in using the advantages and possibilities of the socialist system, its economic power and social potential, in updating the obsolescent social patterns and the style and methods of work, in bringing them abreast of the changed conditions. That is the only way for us to increase the might of our country, to raise the material and spiritual life of the Soviet people to a qualitatively new level, and to enhance the constructive influence of socialism's example as a social system on world development.

We look to the future confidently, because we are clearly aware of our tasks and the ways to carry them out. We look to the future confidently, because we rely on the powerful support of the people. We look to the future confidently, because we are acting in the interests of the socialist fatherland, in the name of the great ideals to which the Communist Party has dedicated itself wholeheartedly.

I. THE CONTEMPORARY WORLD:ITS MAIN TENDENCIES AND CONTRADICTIONS

Comrades, the draft Programme of the Party contains a thorough analysis of the main trends and features of the current development of the world. It is not the purpose of the programme to anticipate the diversity of the concrete developments of the future. That would be a futile occupation. But here is another, no less accurate point: if we want to follow a correct, scientifically grounded policy, we must clearly understand the key tendencies of the current reality. To penetrate deep into the dialectic of the events, into their objective logic, to draw the right conclusions that reflect the motion of the times, is no simple thing, but it is imperatively necessary.

In the days before the October Revolution, referring to the capitalist economy alone, Lenin noted that the sum-total of the changes in all their ramifications could not have been grasped even by seventy Marxes. But, Lenin continued, Marxism has discovered "the *laws*...and *objective* logic of these changes and of their historical development...in its chief and basic features..." *(Collected Works,* Vol. 14, p. 325)

The modern world is complicated, diverse and dynamic, and shot through with contending tendencies and contradictions. It is a world of the most intricate alternatives, anxieties and hopes. Never before has our home on Earth been exposed to such great political and physical stresses. Never before has Man exacted so much tribute from nature, and never has he been so vulnerable to the forces he himself has created.

World developments confirm the fundamental Marxist-Leninist conclusion that the history of society is not a sum of fortuitous elements, that it is not a disorderly 'Brownian motion' but a law-governed onward process. Not only do its contradictions pass sentence on the old world, on everything that impedes the advance; they are also the source, the motive force behind the progress of society in the setting of struggle that is inevitable as long as exploitation and exploiting classes still exist.

The liberation revolutions triggered by the Great October Revolution are determining the image of the 20th century. However considerable the achievements of science and technology, and however great the influence on the life of society of the rapid scientific and technological progress, nothing but the social and spiritual emancipation of Man can make him truly free. And no matter what difficulties, objective and artificial, the old world may occasion, the course of history is irreversible.

The social changes of the century are altering the conditions for the further development of society. New economic, political, scientific, technical, internal and international factors are beginning to operate. The interconnection between states and between peoples is increasing. And all this is setting new, especially rigid, demands upon every state, whether in foreign policy, in economic and social activity, or the spiritual image of society.

The progress of our time is rightly identified with socialism. World socialism is a powerful international entity with a highly developed economy, substantial scientific resources, and a dependable politico-military potential. It accounts for more than one-third of humanity, for dozens of countries and peoples opening up in every way the intellectual and moral wealth of Man and society. A new way of life has taken shape, based on the principles of socialist justice, with neither oppressors nor oppressed, neither exploiters nor exploited, where power belongs to the people. Its distinctive features are collectivism and comradely mutual assistance, triumph of the ideas of freedom, unbreakable unity between the rights and duties of every member of society, the dignity of the individual, and true humanism. Socialism is a realistic option open to all humanity, an example projected into the future.

Socialism sprang up and was built in countries that were far from economically and socially advanced at that time, differing greatly from one another in mode of life and their historical and national traditions. Each one of them advanced to the new social system along its own way, confirming Marx's prediction about the "infinite variations and gradations" of the same economic basis in its concrete manifestations *(Capital,* Vol. III. p. 779).

The way was neither smooth nor simple. It was exceedingly difficult to raise the backward or ruined economy, to teach millions of people to read and write, to provide them with a roof over their heads, with food and free medical aid. The very novelty of the social tasks, the ceaseless military, economic, political and psychological pressure of imperialism, the need for tremendous efforts to ensure defence—all this could not fail to influence the course of events, their character, and the rate at which the socio-economic programmes and transformations were carried into effect. Nor were mistakes in politics, and various subjectivist deviations, avoided.

But such is life; it always takes the shape of diverse contradictions, sometimes quite unexpected ones. This other point is much more important: socialism has demonstrated its ability to resolve social problems on a fundamentally different basis than before, namely a collectivist one, has brought the countries to higher levels of development, and has given the working people a decent and secure life.

Socialism is continuously improving social relations, multiplying its achievements purposefully, building up the impact and credibility of its example, and demonstrating the tangible humanism of the socialist life style. By so doing, it is erecting an increasingly dependable barrier to the ideology and policy of war and militarism, reaction and force, to all forms of man-hating, and is actively furthering social progress. It has grown into a powerful moral and material power, and has shown what opportunities are arising for modern-day civilisation.

The course of social progress is tied in closely with anti-colonial revolutions, national liberation movements, the renascence of quite a few countries, and the emergence of dozens of new ones. Having won political independence, they are working hard to overcome backwardness, poverty, and sometimes desperate misery—the entire painful legacy of their slavish past. They, who were once rightless objects of imperialist policy, are now making history by themselves.

Social progress is expressed in the development of the international communist and working-class movement and in the growth of the new massive democratic movement of our time, including the anti-war and anti-nuclear movement. It is apparent, too, in the stratification of the political forces of the capitalist world, notably the USA the metropolitan centre of imperialism. Here, progressive tendencies are forcing their way forward through a system of monopolistic totalitarianism, exposed to the continuous pressure of organised reactionary forces, including their enormous progaganda machine which loosens avalanches of stupefying misinformation upon people.

Marx compared progress in exploiting society to "that hideous pagan idol, who would not drink but from the skulls of the slain" *(Selected Works,* Vol. 1, p. 499). He amplified: "In our days everything seems pregnant with its contrary. Machinery, gifted with the wonderful power of shortening and fructifying human labour, we behold starving and overworking it. The new-fangled sources of wealth, by some strange weird spell, are turned into sources of want. The victories of art seem bought by the loss of character. At the same pace that mankind masters nature, Man seems to become enslaved to other men or to his own infamy. Even the pure light of science seems unable to shine but on the dark background of ignorance. All our invention and progress seem to result in endowing material forces with intellectual life, and in stultifying human life into a material force" *(Selected Works,* Vol. 1, p. 500).

Marx's analysis is staggering for its historical sweep, accuracy, and depth. It has, indeed, become still more relevant with reference to the bourgeois reality of the 20th century than it was in the 19th. On the one hand, the swift advance of science and technology has opened up unprecedented possibilities for mastering the forces of nature and improving humanity's conditions of life. On the other, the 'enlightened' 20th century is going down in history as a time marked by such imperialist outgrowths as the most devastating wars, an orgy of militarism, fascism, genocide, and the destitution of millions of people. Ignorance and obscurantism go hand in hand in the capitalist world with lofty achievements of science and culture. That is the society we are compelled to be neighbours of, looking for ways of co-operation and mutual understanding. Such is the command of history.

The progress of humanity is also directly connected with the scientific and technological revolution. It matured slowly and gradually, and then, in the final quarter of the century, gave the start to a gigantic accretion of Man's material and spiritual resources. They were of two kinds. A qualitative leap was registered in humanity's productive forces. But there was also a qualitative leap in means of destruction, in military matters, 'endowing' Man for the first time in history with the physical capacity for destroying all life on Earth.

The facets and consequences of the scientific and technological revolution vary in the different socio-political systems. The capitalism of the 1980s, the capitalism of the age of electronics and computer science, computers and robots, is leaving more millions of people, including youth and educated people, without jobs. Wealth and power are being increasingly concentrated in the hands of a few. Militarism is gorging itself on the arms race beyond reason, and also wants to gain control little by little over the political levers of power. It is becoming the ugliest and most dangerous monster of the 20th century. By its efforts, the most advanced scientific and technical ideas are being converted into weapons of mass destruction.

To the developing countries the scientific and technological revolution is setting the most acute question: are they fated to enjoy the achievements of science and technology in full measure in order to gain strength for combating neocolonialism and imperialist exploitation or will they remain on the periphery of world development? The scientific and technological revolution shows in bold relief that many socio-economic problems impeding progress in that part of the world are unresolved.

Socialism has everything it needs to place modern-day science and technology at the service of the people. But it would be wrong to think that the scientific and technological revolution is creating no problems for socialist society. Experience shows that its advance involves improvement and social relations, a change of mentality, the forging of a new psychology, and the acceptance of dynamism as a way of life and a rule of being. It calls insistently for continuous reassessment and renewal of the prevailing patterns of management. In other words, the scientific and technological revolution not only opens up prospects, but also sets higher demands on the entire organisation of home and international affairs. Certainly, scientific and technological progress cannot abolish the laws of social development or the social purpose and content of such development. But it exercises a tremendous influence on all the processes that are going on in the world, on its contradictions.

It is quite obvious that the two socio-economic systems differ substantially in their readiness and also in their capacity to conceptualise and resolve the arising problems.

Such is the world we are living in on the threshold of the third millennium. It is a world full of hope, because people have never before been so amply equipped for the further development of civilisation. But it is also a world overloaded with dangers and contradictions, prompting the thought that this is perhaps the most alarming period in history.

The first and most important group of contradictions in terms of humanity's future is connected with the relations between countries of the two systems, the two formations. These contradictions have a long history. Since the Great October Revolution in Russia and the split of the world on the social-class principle, fundamental distinctions have come to light in the assessment of current affairs and in the views concerning the world's social perspective.

Capitalism regarded the birth of socialism as an 'error' of history which must be 'rectified'. It was to be rectified at any cost, by any means, irrespective of law and morality: by armed intervention, economic blockade, subversive activity, sanctions and 'punishments', or refusal of any and all co-operation. But nothing could interfere with the consolidation of the new system and its historical right to live.

The difficulty that the ruling classes of the capitalist world have in understanding the realities,

The seeing-off ceremony at the Great Kremlin Palace for Algerian President Shadli Bengedid and his wife prior to their departure on March 28, 1986.

In early April 1986 in the Kremlin Gorbachov received the Chairman of the Committee on Foreign Affairs of the House of Representatives of the USA and Congressman W. Broomfield.

the periodical recurrence of attempts at resolving by force the whole group of contradictions dividing the two worlds are, of course, anything but accidental. Imperialism is prompted by its intrinsic mainsprings and socio-economic essence to translate the competition of the two systems into the language of military confrontation. By dint of its social nature, imperialism ceaselessly generates aggressive, adventurist policy.

Here we can speak of a whole complex of impelling motives: the predatory appetites of the arms manufacturers and the influential military-bureaucratic groups, the selfish interest of the monopolies in sources of raw materials and sales markets, the bourgeoisie's fear of the ongoing changes, and lastly the attempts to resolve its own, snow-balling problems at socialism's expense.

The latter are especially typical of U.S. imperialism. It was nothing but imperial ideology and policy, the wish to create the most unfavourable external conditions for socialism and for the USSR that prompted the start of the race of nuclear and other arms after 1945, just when the crushing defeat of fascism and militarism was, it would seem, offering a realistic opportunity for building a world without wars, and a mechanism of international co-operation—the United Nations—had been created for this purpose. But imperialism's nature asserted itself that time again.

Today, too, the right wing of the U.S. monopoly bourgeoisie regards the stoking up of international tensions as something that justifies military allocations, claims to global supremacy, interference in the affairs of other states, and an offensive against the interests and rights of the American working people. No small role seems to be played by the idea of using tensions to exercise pressure on the allies, to make them implicitly obedient, to subordinate them to Washington's dictation.

The policy of total contention, of military confrontation, has no future. Flight into the past is no response to the challenges of the future. It is rather an act of despair which, however, does not make this posture any less dangerous. Washington's deeds will show when and to what extent it will understand this. We, for our part, are ready to do everything we can in order to radically improve the international situation. To achieve this, socialism need not renounce any of its principles or ideals. It has always stood for, and continues to stand for, the peaceful coexistence of states belonging to different social systems.

As distinct from imperialism, which is trying to halt the course of history by force, to regain what it had in the past, socialism has never, of its own free will, related its future to any military solution of international problems. This was borne out at the very first big discussion that took place in our country after the victory of the Great October Revolution. During that discussion, as we may recall, the views of the 'left communists' and the Trotskyites, who championed the theory of 'revolutionary war' which, they claimed, would carry socialism to other countries, were firmly rejected. This position, as Lenin emphasised in 1918, "would be completely at variance with Marxism, for Marxism has always been opposed to 'pushing' revolutions, which develop with the growing acuteness of the class antagonisms that engender revolutions." *(Collected Works,* Vol. 27, pp. 71-72). Today, too, we are firmly convinced that pushing revolutions from outside, and doubly so by military means, is futile and inadmissible.

The problems and crises experienced by the capitalist world arise within its own womb and are a natural result of the internal antagonistic contradictions of the old society. In this sense, capitalism negates itself as it develops. Unable to cope with the acute problems of the declining phase of capitalism's development, the ruling circles of the imperialist countries resort to means and methods that are obviously incapable of saving the society which history has doomed.

The myth of a Soviet or communist 'threat' that is being circulated today, is meant to justify the arms race and the imperialist countries' own aggressiveness. But it is becoming increasingly clear that the path of war can yield no sensible solutions, either international or domestic. The clash and struggle of the opposite approaches to the perspectives of world development have become especially complex in nature. Now that the world has huge nuclear stockpiles and the only thing experts argue about is how many times or dozens of times humanity can be destroyed, it is high time to begin an effective withdrawal from the brink of war, from the equilibrium of fear, to normal, civilised forms of relations between the states of the two systems.

In the years to come, the struggle will evidently centre on the actual content of the policy that can safeguard peace. It will be a hard and many-sided struggle, because we are dealing with a society whose ruling circles refuse to assess the realities of the world and its perspectives in sober terms, or to draw serious conclusions from their own experience and that of the others. All this is an indication of the wear and tear suffered by its internal 'systems of immunity', of its social senility, which reduces the probability of far-reaching changes in the policy of the dominant forces and augments its degree of recklessness.

That is why it is not easy at all, in the current circumstances, to predict the future of the relations between the socialist and the capitalist countries, the USSR and the USA. The decisive factors here will be the correlation of forces on the world scene, the growth and activity of the peace potential, and its capability of effectively repulsing the threat of nuclear war. Much will depend, too, on the degree of realism that Western ruling circles will show in assessing the situation. But it is unfortunate when not only the eyesight but also the soul of politicians is blind. With nuclear war being totally unacceptable, peaceful coexistence rather than confrontation of the systems should be the rule in inter-state relations.

The second group of contradictions consists of the intrinsic contradictions of the capitalist world itself. The past period has amply confirmed that the general crisis of capitalism is growing keener. The capitalism of today, whose exploitative nature has not changed, is in many ways different from what it was in the early and even in the middle 20th century. Under the influence and in the setting of the scientific and technological revolution, the conflict between the productive forces, which have grown to gigantic proportions, and the private-owner social relations, has become still more acute. Here there is growth of unemployment and deterioration of the entire set of social problems. Militarism, which has spread to all areas, is applied as the most promising means of enlivening the economy. The crisis of political institutions, of the entire spiritual sphere, is growing. Reaction is exercising fierce pressure all along the line—in home and foreign policy, economy and culture, and the use of the achievements of human genius. The traditional forms of conservatism are giving place to authoritarian tendencies.

Special mention should be made of anti-communism and anti-Sovietism, a most dangerous aspect of the crisis of capitalism. This concerns not only external policy. In the modern-day system of imperialism it is also a most important area of internal policy, a means of pressure on all the advanced and progressive elements that live and fight in the capitalist countries, in the non-socialist part of the world.

True, the present stage of the general crisis does not lead to any absolute stagnation of capitalism and does not rule out possible growth of its economy and the emergence of new scientific and technical trends. It 'allows for' sustaining concrete economic, military, political and other positions, and in some cases even for possible social revenge, the regaining of what had been lost before. But lacking positive aims and guidelines that would express the interests of the working masses, capitalism now has to cope with an unprecedented interlacement and mutual exacerbation of all groups of its contradictions. It faces so many social and other impasses as it has never known before in all the centuries of its development.

Among the first to grow more acute are the contradictions between labour and capital. In the 1960s and 70s, with the onset of a favourable economic situation, the working class, and the working people generally, managed to secure a certain improvement of their condition. But from the mid-70s on, the proliferating economic crises and another technological modernisation changed the situation, and enabled capital to go on the counter-offensive, depriving the working people of a considerable part of their social gains. For a number of standard of living indicators, the working people were flung many years back. Unemployment has reached a postwar high. The condition of peasants and farmers is deteriorating visibly: some farms are going bankrupt, with their former owners joining the ranks of wage workers, while others become abjectly dependent on large agricultural monopolies and banks. The social stratification is growing deeper and increasingly striking. In the United States, for example, one per cent of the wealthiest families own riches that exceed by nearly 50 per cent the total wealth of 80 per cent of all the American families, who make up the lower part of the property pyramid.

Imperialism's ruling circles are doubtlessly aware that such a situation is fraught with social explosions and political destabilisation. But this is not making their policies more considered. On

A meeting of high Party and State officials of the Warsaw Pact countries took place on April 26, 1985. Here the chiefs of the delegations are shown after signing the protocol.

the contrary, the most irreconcilable reactionary groups of the ruling class have, by and large, taken the upper hand in recent years. The period is marked by an especially massive and brutal offensive of the monopolies on the rights of the working people.

The whole arsenal of means at capitalism's disposal is being put to use. The trade unions are persecuted and economically blackmailed. Anti-labor laws are being enacted. The left and all other progressives are being persecuted. Continuous control or, to be more precise, surveillance of oeople's state of mind and behaviour has become standard. Deliberate cultivation of individualism, of the principle that might is right in the fight for survival, immorality, and hatred of all that is democratic—this is practised on an unprecedented scale.

The future, the working people's fight for their rights, for social progress, will show how the basic contradiction between labour and capital will develop and what conclusions will be drawn from the prevailing situation. But mention must be made of the serious danger to international relations of any further substantial shift of policy, of the entire internal situation in some capitalist countries, to the right. The consequences of such a development are hard to predict, and we must not under-rate their danger.

The last decades of the century are marked by new outbreaks of inter-imperialist contradictions and the appearance of their new forms and tendencies. This group of capitalist contradictions has not been eliminated either by class affinity, the interest in uniting forces, by military, economic and political integration, or by the scientific and technological revolution. The latter has incontestably accelerated the internationalisation of capitalist production, and has given added impetus to the evening up of levels as well as to the leap-like development of capitalist countries The competition that has grown more acute under the impact of scientific and technologica progress, is hitting those who have dropped behind still more mercilessly. The considerable com plication of the conditions of capitalist reproduction, the diversity of crisis processes, and the intensification of international competition have made imperialist rivalry especially acute and bit ter. The commercial and economic struggle in the world market is witnessing ever greater reli ance on the power of national state-monopoly capitalisms, with the role of the bourgeois state becoming increasingly aggressive and egoistic.

The transnational monopoly capital has gained strength rapidly. It is seizing control of, and monopolising, whole branches or spheres of production both on the scale of individual countries and in the world economy as a whole. By the early 80s, the transnational corporations accounted for more than one-third of the industrial production, more than one half of the foreign trade, and nearly 80 per cent of the patents for new machinery and technology in the capitalist world.

The core of the transnational corporations consists of American firms. Their enterprises abroad use an additional army of wage and salary workers equalling half the number of employed in manufacturing in the USA. At present, they produce something like 1.5 trillion dollars worth of goods and services a year, or nearly 40 per cent of aggregate U.S. output.

The size of the 'second economy' of the United States is double or triple that of the economies of such leading West European powers as the FRG, France and Britain, and second only to that of Japan. Today, the biggest U.S. transnational monopolies are empires whose economic activity is comparable to the gross national product of entire countries.

A new knot of contradictions has appeared and is being swiftly tightened between the transnational corporations and the nation-state form of society's political organisation. The transnational corporations are undermining the sovereignty both of developing and of developed capitalist countries. They make active use of state-monopoly regulation when it suits their interests, and come to brutal grips with it when they see the slightest threat to their profits from the actions of bourgeois governments. But for all that, the U.S. transnational supermonopolies are, as a rule, active conductors of state hegemonism and the imperial ambitions of the country's ruling circles.

The relations between the three main centres of present-day imperialism—the USA, Western Europe and Japan—abound in visible and concealed contradictions. The economic, financial and technological superiority which the USA enjoyed over its closest competitors until the end of the 1960s has been put to a serious trial. Western Europe and Japan managed to outdo their American patron in some things, and are also challenging the United States in such a traditional sphere of U.S. hegemony as that of the latest technology.

Gorbachov meeting with Federal Chancellor of Austria Fred Zinovats in April, 1986.

Washington is continuously calling on its allies not to waste their gunpowder on internecine strife. But how are the three centres of modern-day imperialism to share one roof if the Americans themselves, manipulating the dollar and the interest rates, are not loath to fatten their economy at the expense of Western Europe and Japan? Wherever the three imperialist centres manage to coordinate their positions, this is more often than not the effect of American pressure or outright dictation, and works in the interests and aims above all of the United States. This, in turn, sharpens, rather than blunts, the contradictions.

It appears that people are beginning to wonder about this cause-and-effect relationship. For the first time, governments of some Western European countries, the social democratic and liberal parties, and the public at large have begun to openly discuss whether present U.S. policy coincides with Western Europe's notions about its own security and whether the United States is going too far in its claims to 'leadership'. The partners of the United States have had more than one occasion to see that someone else's spectacles cannot substitute for one's own eyes.

The clash of centrifugal and centripetal tendencies will, no doubt, continue as a result of changes in the correlation of forces within the imperialist system. Still, the existing complex of economic, politico-military and other common interests of the three 'centres of power', can hardly be expected to break up in the prevailing conditions of the present-day world. But within the framework of this complex, Washington should not expect unquestioning obedience to U.S. dictation on the part of its allies and competitors, and especially so to the detriment of their own interests.

The specificity of the inter-imperialist contradictions of the current period also encompasses a possible change of their configuration in the coming decades, with the new capitalist 'centres of power' coming on the scene. This will doubtless lead to a further growth of the bulk of contradictions, to their closer interlacement and aggravation.

A new, complex and mobile set of contradictions has taken shape between imperialism and the developing countries and peoples. The liberation of former colonies and semi-colonies was a strong political and ideological blow to the capitalist system. It has ceased to exist in the shape that it assumed in the 19th century and in which it extended into the first half of the 20th. A slow, arduous, but unstoppable process of socio-economic transformations is under way in the life of nations comprising the majority of mankind. This process, which has brought about no few fundamental changes, has also encountered considerable difficulties.

By political manoeuvring, blandishments and blackmail, military threats and intimidation, and all too often by direct interference in the internal affairs of the newly free countries, capitalism has in many ways managed to sustain the earlier relationships of economic dependence. On this basis, imperialism managed to create and adjust the most refined system of neocolonialist exploitation, and to tighten its hold on a considerable number of newly free states.

The consequences of this are tragic. The developing countries with a population of more than two billion have, in effect, become a region of wholesale poverty. In the early 1980s, the per capita income in the newly free countries was, on the whole, less than 10 per cent that of the developed capitalist states. And in the past thirty years, far from shrinking, the gap has grown wider. Nor is it a question of just comparative poverty. There is illiteracy and misery, chronic undernourishment and hunger, appalling child mortality, and epidemics that afflict hundreds of millions of people.

This is a disgrace for civilised humanity! And its culprit is imperialism. Not only from the point of view of history, that is, of colonial plunder on entire continents which left behind a heritage of unbelievable backwardness, but equally in terms of present-day practices. In just the past ten years, the profits squeezed out of the developing countries by U.S. corporations exceeded their inputs fourfold. An in Latin America and the Caribbean, in the same period, the profits of U.S. monopolies were over eight times greater than their inputs.

It is no exaggeration to say that, to a large extent, the imperialist system is still living off the plunder of the developing countries, off their totally merciless exploitation. The forms and methods are changing, but the essence remains. In the United States, for example, a tangible portion of the national income comes from these very sources. The developing countries are being exploited by all the imperialist states, but, unquestionably, U.S. imperialism is doing it with the least consideration for them. Non-equivalent exchange, unequal trade, juggling and abuse of interest rates—the pumps of the transnational corporations are being used to one and the same end. They are adding still more to the poverty and misery of some, and to the wealth of others, and increasing the polarisation in the capitalist world economy.

The distressing condition of the developing countries is a major worldwide problem. This and nothing else is the true source of many of the conflicts in Asia, Africa and Latin America. Such is the truth, however hard the ruling circles of the imperialist powers may invoke the 'hand of Moscow' in order to vindicate their neocolonialist policy and global ambitions.

Take the problem of debts. Together with the profits shipped out yearly from the developing countries, the accumulated debt means just one thing: the prospects of their development have shrunk, and a further deterioration of the already terrible social, economic and other problems is inevitable.

In the existing circumstances, these countries will not, of course, be able to repay their debts. And if no fair solution is devised, the situation is fraught with grave socio-economic and political consequences on the international scene. It would be wrong to say that the imperialist ruling circles are blind to the underlying danger here. But all their concerns boil down to one thing—how to save the present system of enrichment through the exploitation and super-exploitation of the peoples of the developing countries.

This other thing is certain, as well: there is an irrefutable causal connection between the trillion-sized debt of these countries and the more than trillion-sized growth of U.S. military expenditures in the past ten years. The 200-odd billion dollars that are being annually pumped out of the developing countries and the practically equal size of the U.S. military budget in recent years, are no coincidence. That is why militarism has a direct stake in maintaining and tightening the sytem of neocolonial super-exploitation.

It is also obvious that with capitalism's contradictions growing sharper and its sphere of predominance shrinking, neocolonialism is becoming an increasingly important source of resources that provide monopoly capital with the ability for social manoeuvring, reducing social tensions in the leading bourgeois states, and for bribing some sections of the working people. It is a truly extraordinary source, for a worker's hourly rate in the advanced capitalist states is higher, sometimes several times higher, than a day's earnings in the countries of Asia, Africa and Latin America.

All this cannot go on forever. But, of course, no miracle can be expected: the situation is not going to straighten itself out on its own. The military force that the USA is counting on to maintain the status quo, to safeguard the interests of the monopolies and the military-industrial complex, and to prevent any further progressive change in the newly free countries, can only complicate the situation and precipitate new conflicts. The bags of money are liable to become kegs of gunpowder. Sooner or later, in this area too, capitalism will have to choose between the policy of force and shameless plunder, on the one hand, and the opportunity for co-operation on an equitable basis, on the other. The solutions must be radical—in the interest of the peoples of the developing states.

Analysis of yet another group of contradictions—those on a global scale, affecting the very foundations of the existence of civilisation, leads to serious conclusions. This refers first of all to pollution of the environment, the air and oceans, and to the exhaustion of natural resources. The problems are aggrevated not only by excessive loads on the natural systems as a consequence of the scientific and technological revolution, and by the increasing extent of Man's activity. Engels, in his time, foresaw the ill effects of exposing nature to the blind play of market forces. The need for effective international procedures and mechanisms that would make for the rational use of the world's resources as an asset belonging to all humanity is becoming increasingly apparent.

The global problems, affecting all humanity, cannot be resolved by one state or a group of states. This calls for co-operation on a worldwide scale, for close and constructive joint action by the majority of countries. This co-operation must be based on completely equal rights and respect for the sovereignty of each. It must be based on conscientious compliance with accepted commitments and with the standards of international law. Such is the categorical call of the times in which we live.

Gorbachov receiving the delegation of the Socialist Party of Japan (September, 1985).

Capitalism also causes an impoverishment of culture, an erosion of the spiritual values created over the centuries. Nothing elevates Man more than knowledge. But in probably no other period of history has mankind experienced any stronger pressure of falsehood and deceit than it does now. Bourgeois progaganda shovels ingeniously doctored information on people all over the world, imposing thoughts and feelings, and programming a civic and social attitude advantageous to the ruling forces. What knowledge, what values and moral standards are implicit in the information dispensed to the people and in the system of education is, first and foremost, a political problem.

Life itself brings up the question of safeguarding culture, of protecting it from bourgeois corruption and vandalisation. That is one of the most important worldwide tasks. We cannot afford to neglect the long-term psychological and moral consequences of imperialism's current practices in the cultural sphere. Its impoverishment under the onslaught of unbridled commercialisation and the cult of force, the propagation of racism, the propaganda of lowly instincts, of the ways of the criminal world and the 'lower depths' of society, must be, and certainly will be, rejected by mankind.

The problems, as you see comrades, are many, and they are large-scale and intricate. But it is clear that their conceptualism is, on the whole, lagging behind the scope and depth of the current tasks. The imperative condition for success in resolving the topical issues of international life is to reduce the time of search for political understanding and to secure the swiftest possible constructive action.

We are perfectly well aware that not everything by far is within our power and that much will depend on the West, on its leaders' ability to see things in sober perspective at important crossroads of history. The US President said once that if our planet were threatened by a landing from another planet, the USSR and the USA would quickly find a common language. But isn't a nuclear disaster a more tangible danger than a landing of extra-terrestrials? Isn't the ecological threat big enough? Don't all countries have a common stake in finding a sensible and fair approach to the problems of the developing states and peoples?

Lastly, isn't all the experience accumulated by mankind enough to draw perfectly justified practical conclusions today rather than wait until some other crisis breaks out? What does the United States hope to win in the long term by producing doctrines that can no longer fit U.S. security into the modest dimensions of our planet?

To keep in the saddle of history, imperialism is resorting to all possible means. But such a policy is costing the world dearly. The nations are compelled to pay an ever higher price for it. To pay both directly and indirectly. To pay with millions of human lives, with a depletion of national resources, with the waste of gigantic sums of the arms race. With the failure to solve numerous, increasingly difficult problems. And in the long run, perhaps, with the highest possible price.

The U.S. ruling circles are clearly losing their realistic bearings in this far from simple period of history. Aggressive international behaviour, increasing militarisation of politics and thinking, contempt for the interests of others—all this is leading to an inevitable moral and political isolation of U.S. imperialism, widening the abyss between it and the rest of humanity. It is as though the opponents of peace in that country are unaware that when nuclear weapons are at the ready, the time and space for civilisation lose their habitual outlines, and mankind becomes the captive of an accident.

Will the ruling centres of the capitalist world manage to embark on the path of sober, constructive assessments of what is going on? The easiest thing is to say: maybe yes and maybe no. But history denies us the right to make such predictions. We cannot take 'no' for an answer to the question: will mankind survive or not? We say: the progress of society, the life of civilisation, must and will continue.

We say this not only by dint of the optimism that is usual for communists, but by dint of our faith in people's intelligence and common sense. We are realists and are perfectly well aware that the two worlds are divided by very many things, and deeply divided, too. But we also see clearly that the need to resolve most vital problems affecting all humanity must prompt them to interaction, awakening humanity's heretofore unseen powers of self-preservation. And here is the stimulus for solutions commensurate with the realities of our time.

Gorbachov receiving the delegation of the Socialist Party of Japan.

M. S. Gorbachov,
Member of the Politbureau of the CPSU Central Committee, General Secretary of the CPSU Central Committee

G. A. Aliyev,
Member of the Politbureau of the CPSU Central Committee

V. I. Vorotnikov,
Member of the Politbureau of the CPSU Central Committee

V. M. Chebrikov,
Member of the Politbureau of the CPSU Central Committee

E. A. Shevardnadze,
Member of the Politbureau of the CPSU Central Committee

V. V. Shcherbitsky,
Member of the Politbureau of the CPSU Central Committee

N. V. Talyzin,
Alternate Member of the Politbureau of the CPSU Central Committee

A. P. Biryukova,
Secretary of the CPSU Central Committee

A. F. Dobrynin,
Secretary of the CPSU Central Committee

The Members of the Politburo, Alternate Members of the Politburo, and Secretaries of the CPSU as

A. A. Gromyko,
Member of the Politbureau
of the CPSU Central Committee

L. N. Zaikov,
Member of the Politbureau
of the CPSU Central Committee,
Secretary of the CPSU
Central Committee

D. A. Kunayev,
Member of the Politbureau
of the CPSU Central Committee

P. N. Demichev,
Alternate Member of the Politbureau
of the CPSU Central Committee

V. I. Dolgikh,
Alternate Member of the Politbureau
of the CPSU Central Committee,
Secretary of the CPSU
Central Committee

B. N. Yeltsin,
Alternate Member of the Politbureau
of the CPSU Central Committee

M. V. Zimyanin,
Secretary of the CPSU
Central Committee

V. A. Medvedev,
Secretary of the CPSU
Central Committee

V. P. Nikonov,
Secretary of the CPSU
Central Committee

elected by the Plenary Meeting of the Central Committee of the Communist Party of the Soviet Union.

Ye. K. Ligachov,
Member of the Politbureau
of the CPSU Central Committee,
Secretary of the CPSU
Central Committee

N. I. Ryzhkov,
Member of the Politbureau
of the CPSU Central Committee

M. S. Solomentsev,
Member of the Politbureau
of the CPSU Central Committee,
Chairman of the Party Control
Committee under the CPSU
Central Committee

N. N. Slyunkov,
Alternate Member of the Politbureau
of the CPSU Central Committee

S. L. Sokolov,
Alternate Member of the Politbureau
of the CPSU Central Committee

Yu. F. Solovyov,
Alternate Member of the Politbureau
of the CPSU Central Committee

G. P. Razumovsky,
Secretary of the CPSU
Central Committee

A. N. Yakovlev,
Secretary of the CPSU
Central Committee

I. V. Kapitonov,
Chairman of the CPSU
Central Auditing Commission

M. Gorbachov and associates during a trip to Kiev to inspect the model AN-124 aircraft.

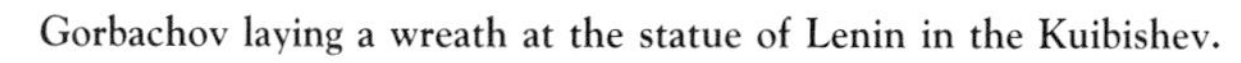

Gorbachov laying a wreath at the statue of Lenin in the Kuibishev.

The course of history, of social progress, requires ever more insistently that there should be constructive and creative interaction between states and peoples on the scale of the entire world. Not only does it so require, but it also creates the requisite political, social and material premises for it.

Such interaction is essential in order to prevent nuclear catastrophe, in order that civilisation could survive. It is essential in order that other worldwide problems that are growing more acute should also be resolved jointly in the interests of all concerned. The prevailing dialectics of present-day development consists in a combination of competition and confrontation between the two systems and in a growing tendency towards interdependence of the countries of the world community. This is precisely the way, through the struggle of opposites, through arduous effort, groping in the dark to some extent, as it were, that the controversial but interdependent and in many ways integral world is taking shape.

The communists have always been aware of the intrinsic complexity and contradictoriness of the paths of social progress. But at the centre of these processes—and this is the chief distinction of the communist world outlook—there unfailingly stands Man, his interests and cares. Human life, the possibilities for its comprehensive development, as Lenin stressed, is of the greatest value; the interests of social development rank above all else. That is what the CPSU takes its bearing from in its practical policy.

As we see it, the main road of march in contemporary conditions is to create worthy, truly human material and spiritual conditions of life for all nations, to see to it that our planet should be habitable, and to deal with its riches rationally. Above all, to deal rationally with the chief value of all—with people and all their potentialities. That is exactly where we offer the capitalist system to compete with us in a setting of lasting peace.

II. THE STRATEGIC COURSE; ACCELERATION OF THE COUNTRY'S SOCIO-ECONOMIC DEVELOPMENT

Comrades, by advancing the strategy of accelerating the country's socio-economic development at the April plenary meeting, the Central Committee of the CPSU adopted a decision of historic significance. It won the wholehearted support of the Party, of the entire people, and is being submitted for discussion at the Congress.

What do we mean by acceleration? First of all, raising the rate of economic growth. But that is not all. In substance it means a new quality of growth: an all-out intensification of production on the basis of scientific and technological progress, a structural reconstruction of the economy, effective forms of management and of organising and stimulating labour.

The policy of acceleration is not confined to changes in the economic field. It envisages an active social policy, a consistent emphasis on the principle of socialist justice. The strategy of acceleration presupposes an improvement of social relations, a renovation of the forms and methods of work of political and ideological institutions, a deepening of socialist democracy, and resolute elimination of inertness, stagnation and conservatism—of everything that is holding back social progress.

The main thing that must ensure us success is the living creativity of the masses, the maximum use of the tremendous potentialities and advantages of the socialist system.

In short, comrades, acceleration of the country's socio-economic development is the key to all our problems: immediate and long-term, economic and social, political and ideological, internal and external. That is the only way a new qualitative condition of Soviet society can and must be achieved.

A. The Results of Socio-Economic Development and the Need for its Acceleration

Comrades, the programme tasks of the Party raised and discussed at our Congress necessitate a broad approach to the assessment of the results of the country's development. In the quarter of a century since the adoption of the third CPSU Programme, the Soviet Union has achieved impressive successes. The fixed production assets of our economy have increased seven times over. Thousands of enterprises have been built, and new industries created. The national income has gone up nearly 300 per cent, industrial production 400, and agricultural 70 per cent.

Before the war and in the early postwar years the level of the US economy appeared to us hard to attain, whereas already in the 1970s we had come substantially closer to it in terms of our scientific, technical and economic potential, and had even surpassed it in output of certain key items.

These achievements are the result of tremendous effort by the people. They have enabled us to enhance considerably the well-being of Soviet citizens. In a quarter of a century real per capita incomes have gone up 160 per cent, and the social consumption funds more than 400 per cent. Fifty-four million flats have been built, which enabled us to improve the living conditions of the majority of families. The transition has been completed to universal secondary education. The number of people who have finished higher educational establishments has increased fourfold. The successes of science, medicine, and culture are universally recognised. The panorama of achievements will not be complete if I say nothing about the deep-going changes in social relations, the relations between nations, and the further development of democracy.

At the same time, difficulties began to build up in the economy in the 1970s, with the rates of economic growth declining visibly. As a result, the targets for economic development set in the CPSU Programme, and even the lower targets of the 9th and 10th five-year plans, were not attained. Neither did we manage to carry out fully the social programme charted for this period. A lag ensued in the material base of science and education, health protection, culture and everyday services.

Certainly, the state of affairs was affected, among other things, by certain factors beyond our control. But they were not decisive. The main thing was that we had failed to produce a timely political assessment of the changed economic situation, that we failed to apprehend the acute and urgent need for converting the economy to intensive methods of development, and for active use of the achievements of scientific and technological progress in the economy. There were many appeals and a lot of talk on this score, but practically no headway was made.

By inertia, the economy continued to develop largely on an extensive basis, with sights set on drawing additional labour and material resources into production. As a result, the rate of growth of labour productivity and certain other efficiency indicators dropped substantially. The attempts to rectify matters by building new plant affected the problem of balance. The economy, which has enormous resources at its disposal, ran into shortages. A gap appeared between the needs of society and the attained level of production, between the effective demand and the supply of goods.

And though efforts have been made of late, we have not succeeded in wholly remedying the situation. The output of most types of industrial and agricultural goods fell short of the targets set by the 26th Congress of the CPSU and the 11th five-year period. There are serious lags in engineering, the oil and coal industries, the electrical engineering industry, in ferrous metals and chemicals, and in captial construction. Neither have the targets been met for the main indicators of efficiency and the improvement of the people's standard of living.

And we, comrades, must draw the most serious lessons from all this.

The first of them may be described as the lesson of truth. A responsible analysis of the past clears the way to the future, whereas a half-truth which shamefully evades the sharp corners holds down the elaboration of realistic policy, and impedes our advance. "Our strength," Lenin said, "lies in stating the truth" *(Collected Works,* Vol. 9, p. 295). That is precisely why the Central Committee deemed it essential to refer once more in the new edition of the Party Programme to the negative processes that had surfaced in the 70s and early 80s. That is why, too, we speak of them at the Congress today.

The other lesson concerns the sense of purpose and resolve in practical actions. The switchover to intensive development of such an enormous economy as ours is no simple matter and calls for considerable effort, time, and the loftiest sense of responsibility. But once transformations are launched, we must not confine ourselves to half-hearted measures. We must act consistently and energetically, and must not hestitate to take the boldest of steps.

And one more lesson—the main one, I might say. The success of any undertaking depends to a decisive degree on how actively and consciously the masses take part in it. To convince broad sections of the working people that the chosen path is correct, to win their interest morally and

Gorbachov laying wreath at the mausoleum of George Dimitrov in Sofia, Bulgaria on October 24, 1985.

materially, and restructure the psychology of the cadre—those are crucial conditions for the acceleration of our growth. The advance will be all the more rapid, the tighter our discipline and organisation will be, and the higher the responsibility of each for his job and its results.

Today, the prime task of the Party and the entire people is to resolutely reverse the unfavourable tendencies in the development of the economy, to impart to it the due dynamism and to give scope to the initiative and creativity of the masses, to truly revolutionary change.

There is no other way. In the absence of accelerated economic growth our social programmes will remain wishful thinking, though, comrades, they cannot be put off. Soviet people must within a short time feel the results of the common effort to cardinally resolve the food problem, to meet the needs for high-quality goods and services, to improve the medical services, housing, the conditions of life, and environmental protection.

The acceleration of socio-economic development will enable us to contribute considerably to the consolidation of world socialism, and will raise to a higher level our co-operation with fraternal countries. It will considerably expand our capacity for economic ties with the peoples of the developing countries, and with countries of the capitalist world. In other words, implementation of the policy of acceleration will have far-reaching consequences for the destiny of our motherland.

B. Economic Policy Guidelines

Comrades, the draft Programme of the CPSU and the draft Guidelines define the main targets of our economic and social development. By the end of this century we intend to increase the national income nearly twofold while doubling the production potential and qualitatively transforming it. Labour productivity will go up by 2.3-2.5 times. energy consumption per rouble of national income will drop by 28.6 per cent and metal consumption by nearly 50 per cent. This will signify a sharp turn towards intensifying production, towards improving quality and effectiveness.

Subsequently, by intensifying these processes we intend to switch over to an economy having a higher level of organisation and effectiveness, with comprehensively developed productive forces, mature socialist relations of production, and a smoothly-functioning economic mechanism. That is our strategic line.

As was emphasised at the conference in the Central Committee of the CPSU in June 1985, the main factors behind this line are scientific and technological progress and a fundamental transformation of society's productive forces. It is impossible to effect cardinal changes with the previous material and technical base. The way out, as we see it, lies in thorough modernisation of the national economy on the basis of the latest scientific and technological advances, breakthroughs on the leading avenues of scientific and technological progress, and restructuring of the economic mechanism and management system.

1. MODERNISATION OF THE NATIONAL ECONOMY ON THE BASIS OF SCIENTIFIC AND TECHNOLOGICAL PROGRESS

The CPSU has a tremendous backlog of experience in carrying out major scientific-technical and socio-economic transformations. However significant they are though, the scales and complexity of the work we carried out in the past cannot be compared with what has to be done in the period ahead to modernize the national economy.

What do we need for this?

First of all, changing the structural and investment policy. The substance of the changes lies in shifting the centre of attention from quantitative indices to quality and efficiency, from intermediate results to final results, from building up production assets to renewing them, from expanding fuel and raw materials resources to making better use of them, and also to speeding up the development of research-intensive industries and of the production and social infrastructures.

A big step forward is to be made in this direction in the current five-year period. It is intended to allocate upwards of 200 billion roubles of capital investments—more than during the past ten years—for modernising and technically re-equipping production. Sizeable though these amounts are, the planning and economic bodies will have to continue the search for additional resources for these purposes.

Large-scale integrated programmes in the strategic areas have been drawn up, and their imple-

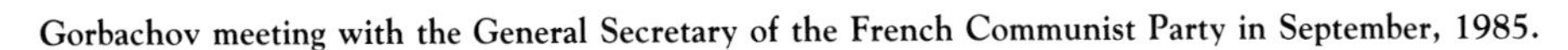

Gorbachov meeting with the General Secretary of the French Communist Party in September, 1985.

mentation has begun.

The industries that play the key role in scientific and technological progress, that assure a quick economic return and the solution of urgent social problems, will move ahead more dynamically. Substantial funds and material, scientific and manpower resources are being concentrated to speed their development.

It is clear that the effectiveness of modernisation and also the economic growth rates depend to a crucial degree on machine-building. This is where the fundamental scientific and technical ideas are materialised, where new implements of labour and machine systems that determine progress in the other branches of the national economy are developed. Here the foundations are laid for a broad advance to basically new, resource-saving technologies, higher productivity of labour and better quality of output.

The Congress delegates know that the CPSU Central Committee and the USSR Council of Ministers recently adopted a decision on the further development of machine-building. In substance, it is a national modernisation programme for this cardinal sector of industry. A single management body has been set up in it. The machine-building complex has been set a goal of sharply raising the technico-economic level and quality of machines, equipment and instruments by the end of the 12th five-year plan period. The capital investments allocated for modernising this industry will be 80 per cent greater than in the previous five years.

What, specifically, do we expect from the implementation of this programme? The output of machinery and equipment is to increase by more than 40 per cent, and their quality standards will be improved. The growing stream of machines of new generations will pave the way for a fundamental retooling of the national economy and a growth in its effectiveness. The resultant annual savings will amount to the labour of about 12 million persons, more than 100 million tons of fuel, and many billions of roubles. Calculations show that use of the Don-1500 harvester combine, for example, will lead to a considerable reduction in the number of grain harvesting machines, will release about 400,000 machine-operators, and will reduce grain losses by millions of tons.

Large-scale introduction of computers and overall automation of production will tremendously influence the rate of technical modernisation. Concrete targets in the development and large-scale production of modern computers and expansion of the manufacture of their components have been defined. The development of computer software and of management information systems has been put on an industrial footing. The Academy of Sciences of the USSR has set up an information science and computer technologies division to coordinate R and D.

Radical modernisation of the fuel and energy complex is the keynote of the Energy Programme. The programme puts the emphasis on energy-saving production methods, on the replacement of liquid fuel by natural gas and coal, and on more sophisticated methods of oil refining. Advanced production methods are also to be employed in the extraction industry: open-cast coal mining, the use of hydromonitors in coal extraction, the development of improved and more reliable oil extraction equipment and the universal introduction of automated systems. In the course of the current five-year span two and a half times more nuclear power plant generating capacities will be started up than in the previous five years, and outmoded units at thermal power stations will be replaced on a large scale.

A great deal will have to be done in the metal-manufacturing and chemical industries, in introducing more highly productive equipment there. The production of fundamentally new and improved structural and other advanced materials will accelerate the growth of electronics, machine-building, construction, and other branches of the economy.

The Party attaches enormous importance to technical re-equipment of the production infrastructure, in the first place in transport and communications. Top priority will be given to the development of the light industry and other industries that directly meet consumer demand. Advanced equipment for them is to be manufactured not only by specialised industries but also by other industries.

We will not be able to carry out technical modernisation unless we radically improve capital construction. This calls for raising the entire building industry complex to a new industrial and organisational level, shortening the investment cycle by a minimum of 50 per cent both in plant modernisation and in the construction of new facilities. We cannot reconcile ourselves any

nger to slow construction rates that freeze enormous sums and retard scientific and technologi-
al progress in the national economy.

All these tasks, comrades, are gigantic in scale and significance. How they are carried out will, the final analysis, determine the fulfilment of our plans and the rates of our growth. Each ctor and each enterprise must have a clear-cut programme for the continuous modernisation of oduction. The responsiblity of the planning and economic bodies for achievement of the anned targets will increase accordingly. Party organisations should also direct their activities wards this.

It is especially important to prevent window dressing and the use of palliative instead of sub-antive measures. There are disquieting instances, and by no means solitary ones, of ministries d departments erecting new facilities under the guise of modernisation, of stuffing them with itdated equipment, and of drawing up costly projects that do not assure the rise of production higher technical-economic levels.

Here is an illustration of that approach. The Bryansk Engineering Works, which puts out mo-rs for diesel locomotives, is now in the middle of a 140-million rouble retooling programme. /hat results will this-modernisation of capacities yield? It turns out that the programme does not ovide for the introduction of progressive technologies, the number of workers has already been creased by nearly 1,000 and the yield per unit of assets has dropped. The worst part of it all is at they intend to use the new capacities to manufacture an outdated motor, although a more ficient model has been designed and tested.

What does the stance of the executives of the Ministry of the Heavy Machine-Building Indus-y and of the Ministry of Railways mean? Evidently some comrades have failed to grasp the pro-und importance of the tasks confronting them. Such examples deserve stern condemnation as ndermining the Party's policy of modernisation and of accelerated scientific and technological rogress. Such cases should be examined with all severity.

The need for modernisation faces scientific research with new tasks. The CPSU will consis-ntly pursue a policy of strengthening the material and technical base of scientific research to e maximum, of providing scientists with the conditions for fruitful work. However, our country entitled to expect from its scientists discoveries and inventions that will bring about genuinely volutionary changes in the development of machinery and production methods.

Important measures to make the work of research establishments more effective have been out-ned lately. They deal with incentives for scientists and new links between science and produc-on. A decision was recently adopted to set up inter-sectoral research-and-technological com-lexes, including large institutes that are the leaders in their respective fields, among them stitutes under academies of sciences, design organisations and pilot plants.

Steps are also being taken to improve the functioning of sectoral research institutes and to crease their contribution to faster scientific and technical progress. However, this process is oing ahead at an impermissibly slow pace. Many institutes are still an appendage of ministry affs: not infrequently they support departmental interests and are bogged down in red tape and aper-work. The question of bringing science closer to production, of including sectoral research stitutes into production and research-and-production associations, was forcefully raised at the ine conference. We must ascertain who is opposing this, what stand the ministries and their arty committees take on the issue, and how they are reacting to life's demands.

The research potential of higher educational establishments must also be used more effectively. Ipwards of 35 per cent of our country's research and educational personnel, including about half f the holders of doctorates, are concentrated there but they carry out no more than ten per ent of the research projects. The respective departments should draft and submit proposals for rengthening the links between university research and production. The proposals should also ke into account the training of the next generation of researchers. Just as a forest cannot live n without new growth, the true scientist is inconceivable without pupils. This is a question of ie future of science, and, therefore, of our country, too. Beginning with their freshman year, ollege and university students should be drawn into research work and into participation in ap-lying research findings in production. This is the only way that real scientists and creatively iinking specialists can be trained.

In sum, comrades, the orientation of science towards the needs of the national economy should be carried out more energetically. However, it is equally important to orient production toward science, to make it maximally receptive to scientific and technological advances. Regrettably, nc few scientific discoveries and major inventions fail to find practical application for years, anc sometimes for decades. I shall cite a few examples.

The non-wear and tear effect, which Soviet scientists discovered three decades ago, led to th development of fundamentally new lubricants that greatly increase the service life of machin parts subjected to friction and sharply reduce labour outlays. This discovery, which yields saving of many millions of roubles, has to this day not yet been applied on a broad-scale because of th blinkers worn by some high-ranking executives of the USSR Ministry of Petrochemical Industr and also of a number of other ministries and departments.

The Ministry of the Motor Vehicle Industry and planning bodies are to blame for the fact tha for about ten years now a newly-invented antifriction bearing, which makes machines more reli able and failure-safe under the most rigorous operational conditions, has not been applied on large scale. The Ministry of the Machine-Tool Industry has impermissibly held up the manufac ture of unique hydraulic motors enabling extensive use of hydraulic techniques in mining anc elsewhere, to increase labour productivity several-fold and to improve working conditions.

Unfortunately, this list could be continued. This kind of attitude to new inventions is no infrequently based on the ambitions of separate groups of scientists, on departmental hostilit towards inventions made 'by others', and a lack of interest on the part of production manager in introducing them. It is no secret that even the examination of invention applications is some times an ordeal that drags on for years.

We cannot reach our targets in accelerating scientific and technological progress unless we fin levers that will guarantee priority only to those research establishments and industrial enterprise whose work collectives actively introduce whatever is new and progressive and seek ways anc means of manufacturing articles of high quality and efficacy.

On February 6, 1986 General Secretary of the CPSU Central Committee Mikhail Gorbachov received ir the Kremlin Senator Edward Kennedy, visiting in the Soviet Union at the invitation of the Supreme Sovie of the USSR.

Gorbachov receiving Prime Minister Rav of North Rhine-Westphalia (West Germany) on September 15, 1985.

We have already accumulated a definite amount of experience in improving the economic mechanism in the sphere of science and its interaction with production. It must be thoroughly analysed and then applied without delay, closely linking up material incentives for research collectives and individual researchers with their actual contributions to the resolving of scientific and technological problems.

All levels of economic management must change their attutude to the introduction of new methods and technology. This also refers to the State Planning Committee of the USSR, which should go over more boldly to all-inclusive planning of scientific and technological progress, as well as to the USSR State Committee for Science and Technology, which is reorganising its work too slowly. The Academy of Sciences of the USSR, ministries and departments should pay more attention to basic research and to applying its findings in production. This is a sacred duty of every scientist, engineer, designer, and manager of an enterprise.

Our activity in the sphere of foreign economic contacts must be tied up more closely with the new tasks. There should be a large-scale, forward-looking approach to mutually advantageous economic relations. The member-countries of the Council for Mutual Economic Assistance have worked out a policy of this kind. It presupposes a switchover in economic relations among them from primarily trade relations to deeper specialisation and co-operation in production, above all in machine-building, and to the establishment of joint associations and research-and-production complexes.

We have no few government departments and organisations that are responsible for separate spheres of foreign economic relations but they do not always coordinate their work. In posing the aim of making active use of foreign economic contacts to speed our development we have in mind a step-by-step restructuring of foreign trade, of making our exports and imports more effective.

2. SOLVING THE FOOD PROBLEM: A TOP PRIORITY TASK

Comrades, a problem we will have to solve in the shortest time possible is that of fully meeting our country's food needs. This is the aim of the Party's present agrarian policy, formulated in the decisions taken by the CPSU Central Committee at its May 1982 plenary meeting and in the Food Programme of the USSR. In the period since their adoption a good deal has been done to expand the material and technical base of agriculture and of the related industries. The economy of the collective farms, state farms, inter-farm enterprises and processing plants has becom stronger; the productivity of crop-farming and livestock farming has risen.

There is progress, but the lag in agriculture is being overcome slowly. A decisive turn is neede in the agrarian sector to improve the food supply noticeably during the 12th five-year plan pe riod. It is planned to more than double the growth rate of farm production and to ensure a sub stantial increase in the per capita consumption of meat, milk, vegetables and fruit.

Can we do this? We can and we must. The Party has therefore worked out additional measure to raise the efficiency of all sectors of the agro-industrial complex. Their substance consists i changing the socio-economic situation in the rural areas, in creating the conditions for greate intensification and guaranteed farm produce. The emphasis is put on economic methods of man agement, broader autonomy of collective farms and state farms and their higher responsibility fo the results of their work.

In carrying out this policy we will have to make more effective use of the production potenti in the agro-industrial complex and concentrate efforts and resources on the most important se tors providing the highest returns. It is a question, first and foremost, of increasing soil fertili and creating the conditions for stable farming. As the experience of recent years has shown, th key to success lies in large-scale application of intensive technologies. They yield a tremendo effect. Their application provided, last year alone, an additional 16 million tons of grain and substantial amount of other produce.

Reducing crop and livestock produce losses during harvesting, transportation, storage and pr cessing is the most immediate source of augmenting food stocks. We have no small potentiali in this respect: the addition to consumption resources could amount to as much as 20 per cen and in the case of some products to as much as 30 per cent. Besides, eliminating the losses wou cost only between a third and one half as much as raising the same amount of produce.

The Central Committee and the government have now defined major steps to reduce losse Rapid expansion of agricultural machine-building will saturate the collective farms and sta farms with highly productive machines capable of performing all the field jobs faster and bette We have also made additional outlays to fortify the manufacture of machinery for the food indu try and facilities for the processing and storage of food.

The Party and the state will continue to persistently enlarge the material and technical ba of the agro-industrial complex. It is equally clear, however, that human beings will, as befo be the mainspring and inspiration of progress. Today, more than ever before, agriculture nee people who want to work actively, who have a high level of professional skill and a feeling the new. Constant attention to the working and living conditions of the members of the ru community is the best guarantee of all our successes. All our plans are geared to this, and it important for them to be carried out unswervingly.

All these are urgent measures, but the programme of action is not confined to them. T switchover of the agrarian sector to new methods of administration and management has to completed. The establishment, in the centre and in the localities, of unified management bod of the agro-industrial complex, called upon to carry out genuine and effective integration of ag culture and of the related industries, is undoubtedly a step of fundamental significance.

The establishment of this organisational framework is backed up by an effective econon mechanism. Proposals on this score have already been drafted. The main idea is to give bro scope to economically viable management methods, to substantially broaden the autonomy collective farms and state farms, to give them a greater incentive and responsibility for the fi results. In substance, it is a question of creatively applying, in the conditions of today, Leni idea of the food tax.

It is intended to establish fixed plans for the purchase of produce from the collective farms a state farms for each year of the five-year period: these plans will not be altered. Simultaneous the farms will be given the opportunity to use, as they see fit, all the produce harvested over a above the plan; in the case of fruit and potatoes and other vegetables they will also be able use a considerable part of the planned produce as they see fit. The farms can sell it addition to the state, can sell it, either fresh or processed, on the collective-farm market or through operative trade outlets, or use it for other needs including the needs of personal subsidiary ho ings. Additional allocations of material resources for which there is a heightened demand, a

ɔ other incentives, will encourage farms to sell grain to the state over and above the plan.
In future, the republics, territories and regions will be given fixed quotas for the supply of pro-ce to centralised stocks: everything produced over and above that will be kept for the local pply system.

There is to be a transition to improved planning methods based on progressive norms. The e of cost accounting will be substantially increased. Past experience shows that neglect of the nciples of self-support, material incentives and responsibility for performance led to a deterio-ion of the financial and economic position of collective farms and state farms and also to their nsiderable indebtedness. Genuine cost accounting, with the incomes of enterprises depending on the ultimate results, should become the rule for all links of the agro-industrial complex, and st and foremost for the collective farms and state farms. The contract and job-by-job systems of yment at the levels of teams, groups and families to whom means of production, including ad, will be assigned for a period specified by contract, will become widespread.

There will be big opportunities for displaying initiative and resourcefulness. This also presup-ses, however, a higher sense of responsibility for meeting the targets of the Food Programme, the results of the financial and economic activity of collective farms, state farms and inter-m enterprises and organisations. A reliable barrier must be erected in the way of mismanage-ent and sponging, and an end must be put to excuses such as "objective circumstances", which me collective farms and state farms have been using to cover up their ineptitude, as well as metimes a lack of desire to work better. The farms will have to use chiefly their own funds to pand production, increase profits and incomes and provide incentives. The practice of provid-g bank loans will have to be substantially altered to stimulate a higher level of activity by col-ctive farms and state farms.

As you see, comrades, rural economic management conditions are undergoing a cardinal ange. This calls for big chances in the style and methods of management in the agro-industrial mplex. An end must be put to imcompetent interference in productive activity in the rural eas. We expect the State Agro-Industrial Committee of the USSR and its local bodies to do erything so that our country receives weighty returns from the measures that are being taken.

ECONOMIC MANAGEMENT MUST MEASURE UP TO THE NEW DEMANDS

omrades, the new economic tasks cannot be solved without an in-depth readjustment of the onomic mechanism, without creating an integral, effective and flexible system of management at will take fuller advantage of the possibilities of socialism.

It is obvious that economic management requires constant improvement. However, the situa-on today is such that we cannot limit ourselves to partial improvements. A radical reform is eeded. Its meaning consists in truly subordinating the whole of our production to the require-ents of society, to the satisfaction of people's needs; in orienting management towards raising ficiency and quality; in accelerating scientific and technological progress; in promoting a greater terest by people in the results of their work, initiative and socialist enterprise in every link of e national economy, and, above all, in the work collectives.

The Central Committee of the CPSU and its Political Bureau have defined guidelines for reor-anising the economic mechanism. We set ourselves the aim of:

-heightening the efficacy of centralised guidance of the economy, strengthening the role of the entre in implementing the main goals of the Party's economic strategy and in determining the tes and proportions of national economic growth, its balanced development. Simultaneously, e practice of interference by the centre in the daily activities of the lower economic links must e overcome;

-resolutely enlarging the framework of the autonomy of associations and enterprises, increasing eir responsibility for attaining the highest ultimate results. Towards this end, to transfer them genuine cost accounting, self-support and self-financing, and to make the income level of col-ctives directly dependent on the efficiency of their work;

-going over to economic methods of guidance at all levels of the national economy, for which urpose to reorganise the system of material and technical supply and improve the system of price rmation, financing and crediting, and working out effective incentives to eliminate over-xpenditure;

-introducing modern organisational management structures, taking into account the trends to-

Gorbachov receiving Zugir Swissi, editor-in-chief of the Algerian weekly magazine *Revolution Africa*.

wards concentration, specialisation and co-operation of production. This is a question of setti up complexes of interconnected industries, research and technological intersectoral centres, va ous forms of economic associations and territorial-production formations;

-ensuring the best possible combination of sectoral and territorial economic management, in grated economic and social development of republics and regions, and the organisation of ratior inter-sectoral contacts;

-carrying out all-round democratisation of management, heightening the part played in it work collectives, strengthening control from below, and ensuring accountancy and publicity the work of economic bodies.

-Comrades, we now unquestionably stand before the most thorough reorganisation of the s cialist economic mechanism. The reorganisation has begun. The direction along which work going ahead in the agro-industrial complex has been spoken about above. Management of t machine-building complex is being upgraded. Industrial enterprises are being transferred, in t main, to a two-level system of management. Beginning with the current year, new econom management methods which have gone through experimental testing have been introduced enterprises and associations that turn out half of the total industrial output. Their introducti in the service sphere, in construction and in transport has begun. Collective forms of work orga isation and stimulation, and also economic contract systems, are being applied on an ever wic scale.

We are only at the beginning of the road, however. Time and energetic efforts are needed reorganise the economic mechanism in our country with its vast and complex economy. Diffic ties may arise, and we are not guaranteed against miscalculations either, but still the main thi now is to move ahead purposefully, step by step, along the direction we have chosen, supp menting and perfecting the economic mechanism on the basis of the accumulated experienc and eliminating everything that has outlived itself or has failed to justify itself.

Success will depend largely on reorganisation of the work of the central economic bodies, fi and foremost the State Planning Committee of the USSR. It must indeed become our countr genuine scientific and economic HQ, freed from current economic matters. We have begun t

, new management bodies of the intersectoral complexes are being set up, and the lion's : of the operational management functions is being delegated directly to the enterprises and :iations. The State Planning Committee and other economic agencies must concentrate their ts on long-range planning, on ensuring proportional and balanced economic development, arrying out the structural policy, and on creating the economic wherewithal and incentives .ttaining the best final results in each unit of the national economy. Considerable improvets are needed in the sphere of statistics.

ıtely there has been a weakening of the financial-credit influence on the economy. The fi:ial system does not sufficiently stimulate higher economic efficacy. The defective practice of me redistribution, with the losses of lagging enterprises, ministries and regions covered at the nse of those that operate profitably, has reached a large scale. This undermines cost account- promotes dependency and prompts endless demands for assistance from the centre. Crediting onger serves its purpose.

Any radical reforms," said Lenin, "will be doomed to failure unless our financial policy is essful." *(Collected Works,* Vol. 27 p. 383.) Accordingly, we must radically change the sub:ce, organisation and methods of the work of the financial and credit bodies. Their chief aim ɔt to carry out petty regulation of the functioning of enterprises but to provide economic ntives and to consolidate money circulation and cost accounting, which is the best possible roller. Everything must be made dependent on the end result.

he question of improving the practice of levying the turnover tax, of deductions from profit other budget revenue has obviously become ripe. The size and procedure of these payments ıld more actively influence the lowering of production costs, the improvement of the quality ıtput and the quickening of its marketing.

rices must become an active factor of economic and social policy. We shall have to carry out anned readjustment of the price system as an integral whole in the interests of organising :tive cost accounting and in conformity with the aims of increasing the real incomes of the ılation. Prices must be made more flexible; price levels must be linked up not only with the

M. Gorbachov visited the "Peugot" car factory in early October, 1985.

outlays but also with the consumer properties of the goods, their effectiveness and the degre which products meet the needs of society and consumer demand. Ceiling prices and cont prices are to be employed more widely.

The system of material and technical supply also needs thorough improvement. It must turned into a flexible economic mechanism which helps the national economy to function rhy mically and steadily. It is the direct duty of the State Committee for Material and Techn Supply to contribute actively to the establishment of direct long-term relations between produ and consumers on a contractual basis, and to improve the observance of the terms of deliv Wholesale trade in means of production should be developed.

In the final analysis, everything we are doing to improve management and planning anc readjust organisational structures is aimed at creating conditions for effective functioning of basic link of the economic system: the association or enterprise.

It is high time to put an end to the practice of ministries and departments exercising p tutelage over enterprises. Ministries should concentrate their attention on technical policy intrasectoral proportions, and on meeting the demands of the national economy in high-gr output by their industries. Enterprises and organisations should be given the right to sell to another, independently, what they produce over and above the plan, raw and other mate and equipment which they do not use, and so on. They should also be given the legal righ make such sales to members of the public. What sense is there in destroying or dumping o waste heaps articles that could come in useful in the household, in building homes, garage bungalows on garden and vegetable allotments?

It would be difficult to overestimate the role of economic norms. When the work collect of enterprises know, ahead of time, specifics of the planned period—delivery targets, prices, ductions from profits to the budget, norms for making up payroll funds and cost-accounting centives funds—they can draw up creatively plans providing for higher growth rates of out and much higher efficiency without being afraid to reveal their as yet untapped potentialit Moreover, enterprises should be given the possibility—following the example of the Volga a works and the Sumy engineering works—to earn, themselves, the funds needed to expand retool production.

It is especially important to give enterprises and organisations greater autonomy in the sph of consumer goods manufacture and services. Their task is to react quickly to consumer dema It is along these lines that we are reshaping the economic mechanism of light industry. The ra of targets approved from above is being sharply limited for enterprises in this sphere: their p grammes will be drawn up chiefly on the basis of contracts with trade organisations, which turn, must see to it that their orders conform to the actual consumer demand. In other wo the quantity, range and quality of goods—that is, just what people need—will be the main th instead of gross output. Besides, it is planned to establish intersectoral production and industr commercial associations for the manufacture and sale of light industry goods and to open n retail outlets operated by them.

The time has come also to solve another problem. The sum of an enterprise's payroll sh be directly tied in with the returns from the sale of its products. This will help to exclude manufacture and supply of low-grade goods for which there is no demand, or, as they say, ope ing for the warehouse. Incidentally, that approach should be applied not only in light indu but in other industries too. We can no longer reconcile ourselves to a situation in which personnel of enterprises producing worthless goods lead an untroubled life, drawing their full and receiving bonuses and other benefits.

A well-thought-out approach must also be taken to the question of a rational combinatio large, medium and small enterprises. As experience shows, small, well-equipped plants have t own advantages in many cases. They can be quicker and more flexible in taking into acc technological innovations and changes in demand, can faster meet the demand for small b and separate items, and can make better use of available manpower, especially in small towr

Another substantial aspect for readjustment is consolidation of the territorial approach to p ning and management. This is specially important for our vast and multinational country its diverse features. The actions of ministries and departments that neglect these features requirements of regions, with resulting economic imbalances, were rightly criticised at Party ferences and at congresses of the Communist Parties of constituent republics.

Some suggestions are also being received on this score. It is evidently worthwhile giving thought to enlarging the powers of republican and local bodies—following the example of the agro-industrial complex—in the management of construction, intersectoral production units, the social and production infrastructures, and many consumer goods factories. The work of the State Planning Committee of the USSR and of the ministries should get a broader territorial orientation. The question of national-economic management on the basis of large economic areas deserves study.

Our short-term and long-range plans are linked, to a considerable degree, with development of the natural wealth of Siberia and the Soviet Far East. This is very important, and a statesman-like approach ensuring integrated regional development should be taken to it. Special attention should be paid to providing people there with the conditions for fruitful work and a full-blooded life. That is the main question today, and fulfillment of the set targets depends on how it is solved.

Attention should be drawn at our Congress to the problems involved in the further socio-economic development of the non-black-earth zone of the Russian Federation. I will stress two points. The Central Committee of the CPSU and the Soviet Government have adopted special decisions for an upswing in non-black-earth zone agriculture, and they must be carried out unswervingly and fully. That is in the first place. And in the second place, the local Party, government and economic bodies and work collectives must pay much more attention to making effective use of the potential accumulated there and also of the allocated resources.

Consolidation of the territorial principle of management calls for a higher level of economic guidance in each republic, region, city and district. Proposals that come from the localities are at times not thought out thoroughly, are not dictated by the interests of the national economy but sooner by a dependant's mentality and sometimes even by self-seeking interests, which draw the economy into capital-intensive but low-productive projects. Due attention is not paid everywhere to raising the efficiency of production. In Kazakhstan, for example, the share of national income per unit of fixed production assets is a third less than the average for the Soviet economy. In Turkmenia, the productivity of social labour has not grown at all in 15 years. Thought should be given to ways and means of tying in social allocations more closely with the efficiency of the regional economy.

Comrades, every readjustment of the economic mechanism begins, as you know, with a readjustment of thinking, with a rejection of old stereotypes of thought and actions, with a clear understanding of the new tasks. This refers primarily to the activity of our economic personnel, to the functionaries of the central links of administration. Most of them have a clear idea of the Party's initiatives, actively support them, boldly tackle complicated assignments, and seek and find the best ways of carrying them out. This attitude deserves utmost support. It is hard, however, to understand those who take a wait-and-see policy or, who, like the Gogol character that thought up all kinds of fanciful ideas, do not actually do anything or change anything. There will be no reconciliation with the stance taken by functionaries of that kind. We will simply have to part ways with them. All the more so do we have to part ways with those who hope that everything will settle down and return to the old lines. That will not happen, comrades!

In our work of restructuring the economy and the economic mechanism it is more important than ever to rely on science. Life prompts us to take a new look at some theoretical ideas and concepts. This refers to such major problems as the interaction of the productive forces and the relations of production, socialist ownership and its economic forms, commodity-money relations, the coordination of centralism with the autonomy of economic organisations, and so on.

Practice has revealed the insolvency of the ideas that under the conditions of socialism the conformity of production relations to the nature of the productive forces is ensured automatically, as it were. In real life, everything is more complicated. Indeed, the socialist relations of production open up broad vistas for development of the productive forces. However, this requires constant improvement of the relations of production. And that means outdated economic management methods must be noticed in good time and replaced by new ones.

The forms of production relations and the economic management and guidance system now in operation took shape, basically, in the conditions of extensive economic development. These gradually grew out of date, began to lose their stimulating effect and in some respects became a brake. We are not striving to change the thrust of the economic mechanism, to overcome its costliness and to orient it towards a higher level of quality and efficiency, acceleration of scientific and technological progress and enhancement of the human factor. This is the main thing that will, in practice, signify further improvement of the socialist relations of production and will provide new scope for growth of the productive forces.

In this work we must not be stopped by long-established ideas, let alone by prejudices. If, for example, it is necessary and justifiable to apply economic norms instead of targets that are sent down as directives, this does not mean a retreat from the principles of planned guidance but only a change in its methods. The same can be applied to the need to broaden the autonomy, initiative and responsibility of associations and enterprises, and to enhance their role as socialist commodity producers.

Unfortunately, there was a widespread view that any change in the economic mechanism should be regarded as being practically a retreat from the principles of socialism. In this connection I should like to emphasise the following socio-economic acceleration and the concrete consolidation of socialism should be the supreme criterion in the improvement of management and also of the entire system of the socialist relations of production.

The aspects of socialist property as the foundation of our social system acquire great relevance. Socialist property has a rich content; it includes a multi-faceted system of relations in the use of the means of production and its results, their distribution among people, collectives, industries and regions of the country, and a whole range of economic interests. This complex of relations requires a definite combination and constant regulation, especially since it is in motion. Unless we gain a deep understanding of these changes in theoretical terms we cannot arrive at correct practical decisions or consequently take prompt steps to mould a true sense of commitment to socialist property.

We must provide the working people with greater incentives for putting the natural riches to the best possible use and multiplying them. How can this be done? It would be naive to imagine that the feeling of ownership can be inculcated by words. A person's attitude towards property is shaped, first and foremost, by the actual conditions in which he has been put, by his possibilities of influencing the organisation of production, and the distribution and use of the results of work. The problem is thus one of further intensifying socialist self-government in the economic sphere.

The role of work collectives in the use of social property must be raised decisively. It is important to carry out unswervingly the principle according to which enterprises and associations are wholly responsible for operating without losses, while the state does not bear any responsibility for their obligations. This is where the substance of cost-accounting lies. You cannot be a master of your country if you are not a real master in your factory or collective farm, in the shop or livestock farm. It is the duty of the work collective to answer for everything, to multiply the social wealth. Multiplication of the social wealth, as well as losses, should affect the income level of every member of the collective.

Also, of course, a reliable barrier is needed against all attempts to extract unearned income from the social property. There are still 'snatchers', persons who do not consider it a crime to steal from their plant everything that comes their way, and there are also sundry bribe-takers and grabbers who do not stop at using their position for selfish purposes. The full force of the law and of public condemnation should be applied to all of them.

Attention should also be paid to the topical problem of regulating socialist property relations as guaranteeing unquestionable priority to the interests of the whole people over the interests of industries and regions. Ministries, departments and territorial bodies are not the owners of means of production but merely institutions of state administration responsible to society for efficient use of the people's wealth. We cannot allow departmental and parochial interests to hinder realisation of the advantages of socialist property.

We also stand for full clarity on the question of co-operative property. It has far from exhausted its possibilities in socialist production, in providing better satisfaction of people's needs. Many collective farms and other co-operative organisations demonstrate effective management. And wherever the need exists, utmost support should be given to the establishment and growth of co-operative enterprises and organisations. They should become widespread in the manufacture and processing of products, in housing construction and in construction on garden and vegetable allotments, and in the sphere of everyday services and trade.

It is also high time to overcome prejudices regarding commodity-money relations and underestimation of these relations in planned economic guidance. Refusal to recognise that they have an active influence on people's incentives for working better and on production efficiency leads to a weakening of the cost-accounting principle and to other undesirable consequences. Conversely, sound commodity-money relations on a socialist basis can create a situation and economic conditions under which the results depend entirely on the standards of the work done by the collective and on the ability and initiative of the managers.

Thus, comrades, we are obliged to assess the situation again and again and to resolutely reorganise everything that has become out of date, that has outlived itself. A profound understanding of this aim by Party activists, and by all personnel, as well as its realisation by the broad masses is indispensable for success, and is the point of departure in the exceptionally important work of building up a new economic mechanism and management system.

4. ACTIVATING UNTAPPED ECONOMIC GROWTH POTENTIALITIES

Comrades, the Party has worked out a strategy of deep-going transformations in the national economy and has begun to effect them. They will undoubtedly enable us to speed up economic growth. As was noted, however, this will require a good deal of time, but we must increase the growth rates at once, today. The specific feature of the 12th five-year plan period consists in retooling the national economy on a new scientific and technological basis while simultaneously stepping up the rates of our advance.

From this there follows the need to mobilise all of our untapped potentialities to the maximum. The most sensible things to start with are those that do not require big outlays but yield quick and tangible returns. This is a matter of economic organisational and socio-psychological factors, of making better use of the production capabilities that have been built up, of making the incentives more effective, of improving the level of organisation and tightening discipline, and of eliminating mismanagement. Our untapped potentialities are at hand, and with a dedicated approach plus good management they promise high returns.

Just look at the capacities in service. The value of our country's fixed production assets exceeds 1.5 trillion roubles, but they are not all being used properly. This refers to a number of industries—to machine-building, heavy industry, the power industry and agriculture.

Failure to meet component delivery obligations is another hindrance. A violation of this kind in one place has a ripple effect throughout the national economy and lowers its efficiency. Jerky production also does tangible damage. It is no secret that at the beginning of the month many plants stand idle longer than they function. But at the end of the month they begin a headlong rush, as a result of which output quality is low. This chronic disease must be eradicated. Strict observance of component delivery obligations is the duty of work collectives and also of management at all levels. We will not be able to achieve our aims unless we bring order into planning and supply, unless we create the necessary stocks, unless we impose higher financial liability at all levels for failure to meet obligations and for spoilage.

There are also great untapped potentialities in the use of manpower. Some economic managers complain of a manpower shortage. I think the complaints are groundless in most cases. If you look into the matter more closely you will see that there is no shortage of labour. But there is a low level of labour productivity, inadequate work organisation and ineffective incentive schemes. Add to this the creation of superfluous jobs by planning and economic bodies. It is a well-known fact that some of our enterprises, design offices and research institutes have considerably larger staffs than their counterparts abroad that have a similar work load.

Once people at enterprises get down in earnest to improving work organisation and incentives, to tightening discipline and setting higher demands they bring to light untapped potentialities that had never been suspected previously. Application of the Shchokino method and the certification of work places convincingly confirm this. When Byelorussian railwaymen went over to a new pay system, with one person doing two or more different jobs, about 12,000 workers were soon freed for jobs in other sectors.

Also, of course, more attention must be paid to production mechanisation and automation. In tackling this problem one does not have to wait for machines and devices to be designed and

Mikhail Gorbachov during an official visit to the United Kingdom before his selection as Secretary General.

made somewhere else. A great deal can be accomplished by using one's own capabilities. For instance, efforts in this direction in Zaporozhye Region led, in three years, to a nine per cent reduction in the number of workers employed in manual jobs in industry and a fifteen per cent reduction of those in similar jobs in the building trades. I think that other regions, territories and republics have similar possibilities. The important thing is to put persistent and dedicated effort into this, showing consideration for the people who have to perform manual operations, and striving to reduce production outlays.

Generally speaking, comrades, there are enormous untapped economic potentialities. We have not yet really begun to use many of them. The mentality of a substantial section of the managerial personnel at various levels took shape against the background of an abundance of resources. Many were spoiled by these riches, and that led to wastefulness. However, the situation changed long ago. The former influx of manpower has dwindled, and we have begun to pay a heavy price for every ton of oil, ore and coal we extract and deliver. We cannot close our eyes to these facts; we must reckon with them. We must economise everywhere and always: on the job and at home. We must not ignore mismanagement and wastefulness. Nearly the whole of this year's growth in the national income is to come from raising labour productivity and lowering materials and energy consumption.

That is not simple but wholly feasible. All the more so since our country has accumulated experience in making thrifty use of resources; but it is not being spread fast enough. Party, YCL and trade union organisations should constantly promote: thrift and encourage those who make economical and rational use of raw materials, electrical energy, and fuel. We must make it a firm rule that overexpenditure of resources is disadvantageous and savings are tangibly rewarded.

I would like to put special emphasis on the problem of output quality standards. This is more than our immediate and major untapped potentiality. Accelerated scientific and technological progress is impossible today without high quality standards. We are sustaining large material and moral losses because of flaws in design, deviations from production methods, the use of low-grade materials and poor finishing. This affects the precision and reliability of machines and instruments and hinders satisfaction of consumer demand for goods and services. Last year millions of metres of fabrics, millions of pairs of leather footwear and many other consumer items were returned to factories or marked down as inferior-grade goods. The losses are significant: wasted raw materials and the wasted labour of hundreds of thousands of workers. Radical measures must be taken to rule out the manufacture of defective or low-grade goods.

Not long ago the Central Committee of the CPSU called upon Party committees, government and economic bodies, trade union and YCL organisations and all working people to make maximum efforts to radically improve the quality of goods. This must be a matter of concern for every communist, for every Soviet citizen, for all who respect their own work, for all who cherish the honour of their enterprise, their industry, and the honour of our country.

A great deal of important and intensive work lies ahead of us. The first year of the five-year plan period is a year for persistent work, a year of tests for every manager and work collective. We must come through this test, we must draw all the untapped economic potentialities into production, and consolidate the foundation for further transformations.

The industry and talent of Soviet citizens are the key to attaining the goal that has been set. It is now up to efficient organisation and precise direction of this great force. The part to be played by socialist emulation in this effort cannot be overestimated. It should be spearheaded at raising the standards of work, economising and thriftiness, and reaching the targets set before each collective and at each work place. Enthusiasm and the growing skills have been and, we are confident, will be in future as well, our reliable support.

C. The Basic Guidelines of Social Policy

Comrades, questions of social policy, concern for Man's welfare, has always stood at the centre of our Party's attention.

The social sphere encompasses the interests of classes and social groups, nations and nationalities, the relationship between society and individual, the conditions of work and life, health and leisure. It is the sphere in which the results of economic activity affecting the vital interests of the working people are realised, and the loftiest aims of socialism are carried into effect. It is the sphere in which the humanism of the socialist system, its qualitative difference from capitalism, is seen most distinctly and graphically.

Socialism has eliminated the main source of social injustice—the exploitation of man by man, and inequality in relation to the means of production. Social justice reigns in all areas of socialist social relations. It is embodied in the real power of the people and the equality of all citizens before the law, the actual equality of nations, respect for the individual, and conditions for the all-round development of the personality. It is embodied in this and in broad social guarantees—the right to work, access to education, culture, medical care and housing, concern for people in old age, and mother and child welfare. Strict observance in life of the principle of social justice is an important condition for the unity of the people, for society's political stability and dynamic development.

But life, as they say, does not stand still. So we must look at the further development of the social sphere with new eyes, and appreciate the full measure of its increasing significance. We are committed to doing so by the general course worked out by the Party for the acceleration of socio-economic development, and by the programme aim of our Party, that of achieving the complete well being and a free all-round development of all members of society.

Lessons of the past, too, require that we pay enhanced attention to social issues. The Party's Central Committee holds that central and local bodies had underestimated relevant problems concerning the material base of the country's social and cultural sphere. As a result, in substance a residual principle had taken shape governing allocation of resources for its development. There was a certain overemphasis on technocratic approaches, blunting attention to the social aspect of production, to everyday life, and leisure; this did not fail to reduce the stake that the working people had in results of their work, to slacken discipline, and to lead to other negative developments.

We are not at all indifferent to what ways and means are used to improve the material and spiritual aspects of life and what social consequences this entails. If private-owner, parasitic sentiments, and levelling tendencies begin to surface, this means that something is wrong about the choice of ways and means in our work, and has got to be rectified. During the discussion of the pre-Congress documents, Party members and non-members spoke with concern of the slackening of control over the measure of labour and consumption, of irregularities as regards socialist justice, and of the need for stepping up the fight against unearned incomes. The gravity and importance of these questions is more than obvious.

In short, the attained level of development and the magnitude of the new tasks call for a long-term, deeply considered, integral and strong social policy that would extend to all aspects of the life of society. A resolute turn is essential for the bodies of planning and management, for central and local economic organisations, to face up to the needs of the social sphere.

The objectives of social policy are thoroughly characterised in the drafts of the Party Programme and the Guidelines. Allow me to dwell on some issues related to its implementation.

1. STEADY ENHANCEMENT OF THE PEOPLE'S STANDARD OF LIVING, CONSISTENT ASSERTION OF SOCIAL JUSTICE

The long-term plans for the country's social and economic development envisage raising the people's well being, to a qualitatively new level. In the coming fifteen years, the volume of resources allocated for the improvement of the conditions of life is to be doubled. Real per capita incomes are to go up 60 to 80 per cent. The rise in incomes in the 12th five-year period is to cover millions of people. Huge funds are being earmarked for increasing the construction of homes, and of social and cultural facilities. Those are the plans. But we must mention the main thing: these plans will become reality only if every Soviet person works hard and efficiently. This applies to every person wherever he may work and whatever post he may occupy. What we accomplish is what we are going to have, and how we are going to live.

At election meetings and conferences, communists have rightly raised the question of improving the moral incentives, and indeed of greatly enhancing material incentives, of instilling due order in this important matter. It was rightly pointed out that the so-called 'figure juggling', payment of unearned money, issue of unmerited bonuses, and setting 'guaranteed' pay rates unrelated to the workers's contributed work, is impermissible. It should be said quite emphatically on this score that when equal payments are fixed for the work of a good employee and that of a negligent

Mikhail Gorbachov shakes the hand of the newly appointed Foreign Minister, Edward Shevardnadze on July 2, 1985.

one—that is a gross violation of our principles. And first of all it is an intolerable distortion of socialism's basic principle: 'from each according to his ability, to each according to his work', which expresses the substance of the social justice of the new social system.

Rates and salaries in the non-productive sphere will go up, drawing on centralised sources. A phased increase of the salaries of doctors and other medical workers was started last year. The increase of the rates and salaries of those employed in public education is to be completed in 1987, and a start is to be made that year in raising the salaries of cultural workers. Measures are being taken to extend the wage and salary advantages of factory and office workers in certain regions of Eastern Siberia and the Soviet Far East.

Many proposals made by working people refer to the role of social consumption funds in enforcing the principle of justice. These funds already account for nearly one-third of the consumed material goods and services. We hold that they are in no way charity. They play an important role in proving equal access for members of society to education and culture, and in equalising conditions for the raising of children, and easing the life of those who may, for one reason or another, need a grant or continuous assistance. At the same time, it is a means of encouraging and stimulating qualified, conscientious work. The Party intends to continue promoting the further growth and more effective use of these public funds. In the 12th five-year period they are to go up by 20 to 23 per cent.

Combatting unearned incomes is an important function of the socialist state. We must admit today that owing to a slackening of control and for a number of other reasons groups of people have appeared with a distinct proprietary mentality and a scornful attitude to the interests of society.

Working people have legitimately raised the question of rooting out such things. The Central Committee agrees completely with these demands. It is considered necessary, in the immediate future, to carry out additional measures against parasites, plunderers of socialist property, bribe-takers and all those who embarked on a path foreign to the work-oriented nature of our system. We should also give thought to proposals about perfecting our tax policy, including the institution of a progressive inheritance tax.

But while combatting unearned incomes, we must not permit any shadow to fall on those who do honest work to earn a supplementary income. What is more, the state will promote various forms of satisfying popular demand and providing services. We must attentively examine proposals for regulating individual labour. It stands to reason that such labour must be fully aligned with socialist economic principles, and repose on either co-operative principles or on contracts with socialist enterprises. Society, the population, only stands to gain from this.

All the efforts to perfect the distributive relations will have little effect and the objective of enhancing the people's well being will not be attained if we fail to saturate the market with diverse goods and services. That, indeed, is the purpose of the comprehensive programme for the development of the production of consumer goods and services.

We must build up an up-to-date services industry as quickly as possible. That is the job of central organisations, but also—no less, and perhaps even more—of the councils of ministers of union republics, and all bodies of local government. Resolute measures must be taken to eliminate the glaring disproportions between the supply and demand of services. This applies first of all to services that lighten domestic work and those connected with the improvement and renovation of flats, with tourism, and the servicing of cars—the demand for which is increasing at an especially swift rate. Responding to the proposals of the working people, we are promoting broad expansion of collective gardening and vegetable growing. This has got off the ground. But the work must be continued, and all artificial hindrances have got to be removed.

The social importance and acuteness of the housing problem has predetermined our earnest attitude to it. To provide every family with a separate flat or house by the year 2000 is, in itself, a tremendous but feasible undertaking. In the current five years, and especially in the five-year periods to follow, the scale of house-building and of modernising available housing will increase. The building of co-operative and individual housing should be encouraged in every way. Here we see great untapped potentialities for expanding the building of homes. Those who are backing the construction of youth complexes are doing the right thing. The motivation and energy of young people can do a lot in this respect.

Much is being said about the need for seriously improving the practice of distributing housing. These questions must be settled on a broad democratic basis and put under continuous public control. Proposals for fair changes in the system of house rents by gearing them to the size and quality of all the occupied living space merit attention. There have been many complaints about the low quality of house-building. It is essential to work out measures that would stimulate a substantial improvement of quality, and also an improvement of the layout, the amenities and architecture of our towns and villages.

Comrades, the qualitative changes in the social sphere are impossible without deep-going changes in the content of labour. The main role here is to be played by the technical reconstruction of the economy: mechanisation, automation, computerisation and robotisation which, as I want to stress specially, must have an explicitly clear social orientation. The further change of labour in the setting of the scientific and technological revolution sets high demands on education and the professional training of people. In substance, the task of establishing a single system of continuous education is now on the order of the day.

In recent years, the Central Committee has taken important steps in that direction. A reform has been launched of the general and vocational school. It should be said that the rate and extent of the measures taken under the reform are not satisfactory as yet. A more profound approach is required to the study of the scientific pillars of contemporary production and of the leading trends of its intensification. And what is especially urgent is that all pupils should learn the use of computers. In sum, it is essential that the Leninist principle of combining education with productive labour should be carried into effect more fully, that more radical improvements should be achieved in the results of education, in the training of young people for independent life and labour, and in bringing up politically conscious builders of the new society.

The Party is setting the task of restructuring higher and specialised secondary education. In recent years, the growing output of specialists was not accompanied by the requisite improvement in the quality of their training. The material base of the higher school is lagging behind gravely. The use of engineers and technicians must be considerably improved.

At present, proposals have been drawn up to alter the prevailing situation. It is in the interests of society to heighten the prestige of the work of engineers. The structure of higher and specialised secondary education is to be revised, so that the training of specialists will be abreast of the times and so that they acquire substantial theoretical knowledge and practical skills. The relationship of higher and specialized secondary schools with various branches of the economy should evidently follow new lines, and their mutual stake in raising the level of training and retraining of cadres, in cardinally improving their use in production, should be enhanced.

Nothing is more valuable to every person and, for that matter, to society than health. The protection and improvement of the health of people is a matter of cardinal importance. We must consider the problems of health from broad social positions. Health depends above all on the conditions of work and life, and on the standard of living. It stands to reason, of course, that the public health service is also of tremendous importance. We must meet the needs of the population in high-quality medical treatment, health protection and pharmaceuticals as quickly as possible, and moreover everywhere. All this puts the question of the material and technical base of the health service in a new way, calling for the resolution of many urgent scientific, organisational and personnel problems. Considerable funds will be needed, of course, and we must see to it that they are made available.

It has long since been noted, and most aptly, that health cannot be bought in a pharmacy. The main thing is a person's way of life and, among other things, how sensibly and wholesomely a person uses his or her spare time. The opportunities for this are at hand, but the organisational side of the matter is very poorly run. Much depends on the initiative of the public, on what people do off their own bat. But in towns and villages, and within work collectives, they often wait for instructions and count on assistance from above. Why do we make poor use of what is already at our disposal—of palaces, clubs, stadiums, parks and many other facilities? Why don't the soviets, the trade unions and the Komsomol tackle these questions properly? Why not start a movement for more active building of simple playgrounds and gymnasiums on the residential principle? And finally, why not organise sports, tourist and other clubs on a co-operative basis?

A fight has been mounted across the country against hard drinking and alcoholism. In the name of the health of society and the individual we have instituted resolute measures and started a battle against traditions that were shaped and cultivated over the centuries. While we should have no illusions about what has been accomplished, we can safely say that drunkenness has been elbowed out of factories and that there is less of it in public places. The situation within families is improving, injuries in production have declined, and order has been tightened. But extensive, persevering and varied efforts are still needed to secure a final break with prevailing habits. There must be no indulgence here!

We face the acute task of ensuring the protection of nature and rational use of its resources. Socialism with its plan-governed organisation of production and humane world outlook is quite capable of imparting harmony to the relationship between society and nature. A system of measures to that effect has already been implemented in our country, and quite considerable funds are being allocated for this purpose. There are also practical results.

Still, in a number of regions the state of the environment is alarming. And the public, notably our writers, are quite right in calling for a more careful treatment of land, its bowels, lakes and rivers, and the plant and animal world.

Scientific and technical achievements are being much too slowly introduced in nature protection. The projects of new and the reconstruction of operating enterprises are still being based on outdated notions, with wasteless and low-waste production techniques being introduced on too small a scale. During the processing of minerals, most of the extracted mass goes to waste, polluting the environment. More resolute economic, legal and education measures are required here. All of us living today are accountable for nature to our descendants and to history.

2. IMPROVEMENT OF SOCIAL-CLASS RELATIONS AND RELATIONS AMONG THE PEOPLES OF THE USSR

Comrades, analysing problems involved in interrelationship of classes and social groups is of vital importance for a Marxist-Leninist Party. By carefully taking into account both the community and the specific character of their interests in its policy, the Communist Party ensures society's dependable unity and successful fulfilment of its most important and complex tasks.

The working class holds a vanguard place in Societ society. Owing to its position in the socialist production system, its political experience, high political awareness, good organisation, labour and political activity, the working class unites our society and plays the leading role in improving socialism, in communist construction. Constant concern for the consolidation of the alliance of the working class, the peasantry and the intelligentsia is the cornerstone of the policy pursued by the Communist Party of the Soviet Union. This enables us to muster forces for the speedy solution of the economic and social tasks we have set ourselves.

The unity of socialist society by no means implies a levelling of public life. Socialism fosters the diversity of people's interests, requirements and abilities, and vigorously supports the initiative of social organisations that express this variety. Moreover, socialism needs this diversity, which it regards as an essential condition for the further promotion of people's creative activity and initiative, and the competition of minds and talents, without which the socialist way of life and the onward march would be inconceivable.

Generally speaking, the problem is as follows: unless we elevate production and economic emulation to a new, incomparably higher level, unless we encourage emulation in science and the arts, we shall not be able to cope with the task of accelerating the country's socio-economic progress.

The problems of consolidating the family are attracting public attention. Our achievements in cultivating the new, socialist type of family are indisputable. Socialism has emancipated women from economic and social oppression, securing for them the opportunity to work, obtain an education and participate in public life on an equal footing with men. The socialist family is based on the full equality of men and women and their equal responsibility for the family.

Yet, the formation of the new type of family is no simple matter. It is a complicated process that involves many problems. In particular, although the divorce rate has dropped in the past few years, it is still high. There is still a large number of unhappy families. All this has a negative effect, above all on the upbringing of children, as well as on the morale of men and women, on their labour and public activity. It stands to reason that society cannot be indifferent to such phenomena. The strong family is one of its principal pillars.

Young families need special care. Young people must be well trained for family life. More thought should be given to the system of material assistance to newly-weds, above all in solving their housing and everyday problems. It would apparently be a good thing to consider the proposals for improving relevant legislation with a view to heightening the citizens' responsibility for consolidating the family. But that is not the only point. We have to structure the practical work of governmental bodies and mass organisations so that it would in every possible way help to consolidate the family and its foundations. This means creating conditions for joint public celebrations and cultural and sports outings, for family recreation. It is necessary to honour families with a succession of generations having worked in the same trade, support good family traditions, and use the experience of senior generations in bringing up young people. Here a large, useful contribution could be made by the mass media, television, literature, films and the theatre.

Securing living and working conditions for women that would enable them to successfully combine their maternal duties with active involvement in labour and public activity is a prerequisite for solving many family problems. In the 12th five-year period we are planning to extend the practice of letting women work a shorter day or week, or to work at home. Mothers will have paid leaves until their babies are 18 months old. The number of paid days-off granted to mothers to care for sick children will be increased. The lower-income families with children of up to 12 years of age will receive child allowances. We intend to fully satisfy the people's need for pre-school children's institutions within the next few years.

Thought should also be given to appropriate organisational forms. Why not reinstitute women's councils within work collectives or residentially, integrating them in a single system with the Soviet Women's Committee at its head? Women's councils could help to resolve a wide range of social problems arising in the life of our society.

Concern for the older generation, for war and labour veterans, should rank as one of the top priorities. The Party and the Soviet Government will do everything possible for the pensioners' wellbeing to rise with the growth of society's prosperity. In the 12th five-year period it is planned to increase the minimum old-age, disability and loss-of-breadwinner pensions paid to factory and office workers and to raise the previously fixed pensions of collective farmers. But man lives not by bread alone, as the saying goes. According to the information reaching the Central Committee, many retired veterans feel left out in the cold, as it were. Apparently, additional measures should be taken by government and non-government organisations, centrally and locally, to assist the veterans in becoming more actively involved in production and socio-political life.

The setting up of a national mass organisation of war and labour veterans could be a new step in this direction. It could be instrumental in involving highly experienced people in social and political affairs, and first of all in educating the rising generation. The pensioners' involvement, both on a co-operative and on an individual, family basis, in services or trade, producing consumer goods or turning out farm produce could be highly useful. The new organisation could be helpful in improving everyday and medical services for pensioners and enhancing their leisure opportunities. As we see it, it will certainly have a lot of work to do.

Comrades, of tremendous importance for the multinational Soviet State is to upgrade relations among the peoples of the USSR. The foundation for solving the nationalities problem in our country was laid by the Great October Socialist Revolution. Relying on Lenin's doctrine and on the gains of socialism the Communist Party has done gigantic transformative work in this area. Its results are an outstanding gain of socialism which has enriched world civilisation. National oppression and inequality of all types and forms have been done away with once and for all. The indissoluble friendship among nations and respect for the national culture and dignity of all peoples have taken firm root in the minds of tens of millions of people. The Soviet people is a qualitatively new social and international community, cemented by the same economic interests, ideology and political goals.

However, our achievements must not create the impression that there are no problems in the national interests. Contradictions are inherent in any kind of development, and are unavoidable in this sphere as well. The main thing is to see their emergent aspects and facets, to search for and give prompt and correct answers to questions posed by life. This is all the more important because the tendency towards national isolation, localism and parasitism still persist and make themselves felt quite painfully at times.

In elaborating guidelines for a long-term nationalities policy, it is especially important to see to it that the republics' contribution to the development of an integrated national economic complex should match their grown economic and spiritual potential. It is in the supreme interests of our multinational state, and each of the republics, to promote co-operation in production, collaboration and mutual assistance among the republics. It is the task of Party organisations and the soviets to make the fullest possible use of available potentialities in the common interest and to persistently overcome all signs of localism.

We are legitimately proud of the achievements of the multinational Soviet socialist culture. By drawing on the wealth of national forms and colours, it is developing into a unique phenomenon in world culture. However, the healthy interest in all that is valuable in each national culture must by no means degenerate into attempts to isolate oneself from the objective process by which national cultures interact and come closer together. This applies, among other things, to certain works of literature and art and scholarly writings where, under the guise of national originality, attempts are made to depict in idyllic tones reactionary nationalist and religious survivals contrary to our ideology, the socialist way of life and our scientific world outlook.

Our Party's tradition traceable to Lenin of being particularly circumspect and tactful in all that concerns the nationalities policy and the interests of every nation or nationality, national feelings, call at the same time for resolute struggle against national narrow-mindedness and arrogance, nationalism and chauvinism, no matter what their guise may be. We communists must unswervingly follow Lenin's sage behests, must creatively apply them to new conditions, and be extremely heedful and principled as regards relations among peoples in the name of the further consolidation of fraternal friendship among all the peoples of the USSR.

The social policy elaborated by the Party has many aspects to it and is quite feasible. However, its success will largely hinge on the societal awareness of the cadres, on persistence and initiative in carrying out our plans. Concern for people's needs and interests must be an objective of unflagging attention on the part of the Party, government and economic organisations, of trade unions and each executive. If we succeed in securing a decisive switch to the social sphere, many of the problems that face us today and will face us tomorrow will be solved far more quickly and much more effectively than has so far been the case.

III. FURTHER DEMOCRATISATION OF SOCIETY AND PROMOTION OF THE PEOPLE'S SOCIALIST SELF-GOVERNMENT

Comrades, Lenin regarded democracy, the creative initiative of working people, as the principal force behind the development of the new system. Incomparable in his faith in the people, he showed concern for raising the level of the political activity and culture of the masses, stressing that illiterate people were outside politics. Nearly seventy years have elapsed since then. The general educational and cultural level of Soviet people has risen immeasurably and their socio-political experience has grown richer. This means that the possibility and need for every citizen to participate in managing the affairs of the state and society have grown enormously.

Democracy is the wholesome and pure air without which a socialist public organism cannot live a full-blooded life. Hence, when we say that socialism's mighty potential is not being used to the full in our country, we mean that the acceleration of society's development is inconceivable and impossible without a further development of all the aspects and manifestations of socialist democracy.

Bearing that in mind, the Party and its Central Committee are taking measures aimed at enhancing the democratic character of the socialist system. Among them are steps to invigorate the soviets, the trade unions, the Komsomol, the work collectives and the people's control bodies, and to promote publicity. But all that has been and is being done should be assessed in terms of the scale and complexity of our new tasks, rather than by yesterday's standards. As stressed in the new edition of the Party Programme, these tasks call for consistent and unswerving furtherance of the people's socialist self-government.

In socialist society, particularly under the present circumstances, government should not be the privilege of a narrow circle of professionals. We know from our extensive experience as well as theory that the socialist system can develop successfully only when the people really run their own affairs, when millions of people are involved in political life. This is what the working people's self-government amounts to, as Lenin saw it. It is the essence of Soviet power. The elements of self-government develop within rather than outside our statehood, increasingly penetrating all aspects of state and public life, enriching the content of democratic centralism and strengthening its socialist character.

The Party is the guiding force and the principal guarantor of the development of socialist self-government. Playing the leading role in society, the Party is itself the highest form of a self-governing socio-political organisation. By promoting inner-party democracy and enhancing the activity of communists at all levels of the political system, the CPSU sets the right direction for the process of furthering the people's socialist self-government and broadening the participation of the masses and of each person in the affairs of the country.

The result of the revolutionary creativity of the working people, the soviets of people's deputies have stood the test of time, displaying their viability and vast potentialities in securing full power for the people, in uniting and mobilising the masses. The very logic of the development of socialist democracy speaks of the urgent need for making the maximum use of these potentialities of soviet representative bodies.

That the Supreme Soviet of the USSR and the supreme soviets of the union and autonomous republics are becoming increasingly business-like and effective in their activity with the passage of time is most welcome. It is their duty to progressively improve legislation, supervise law enforcement and check on the actual outcome of the work done by each state body and each executive. At their sessions, the supreme soviets should lay greater emphasis on discussing proposals submitted by trade unions, the Komsomol and other social organisations, the reports of administrative bodies, the situation in different branches of the economy, and the development of the various regions.

I should like to draw the special attention of Congress delegates to the activity of local soviets. Today they can and must serve as one of the most effective means of mobilising the masses for the effort to accelerate the country's socio-economic development. As they receive the electorate's mandate, local government bodies undertake responsibility for all aspects of life on their territory. If someone may be allowed to say "this is none of my business", this approach is certainly unacceptable to the soviets. Housing and education, public health and consumer goods, trade and services, public transport and the protection of nature are all paramount concerns of the soviets. Whenever we hear complaints from working people on these subjects, and that is still fairly frequent, it means that they are lacking efficiency and initiative, and that their control is slack. But while making legitimate demands on the soviets, we should not be blind to the fact that for the time being their ability to tackle many of the local problems is limited; there exists excessive centralisation in such matters which are not always clearly visible from the centre and can be much better solved locally.

That is why we have resolutely set our sights on promoting the autonomy and activity of local government bodies. Proposals to this effect are currently being worked out by the CPSU Central Committee, the Presidium of the Supreme Soviet and the USSR Council of Ministers. Their goal is to make each soviet a full and responsible master in all things related to meeting people's everyday needs and requirements, in using the allocated funds, the local potentialities and reserves, coordinating and supervising the work of all organisations as concerns servicing the population. In this connection, we must make a thorough examination of the relationship between soviets and the centrally-managed enterprises in their territories, and enhance the local bodies' concern for the results of their work.

The sessions of soviets should be conducted in a far more effective way, the analytical and supervisory activity of standing committees should be more thorough, and the practice of deputies' enquiries should be broadened. The committees' recommendations and the deputies' proposals and observations should be carefully considered and taken into account by the executive bodies.

While mapping out further improvements of the work of the soviets, we should remember that none of them will yield the desired results unless backed by the deputies' initiative. The Party will continue to see to it that deputies are elected from among the worthiest people who are capable of effectively running state affairs, and that the soviets' membership should be systematically renewed. It is high time necessary corrections were made in our election procedures. There is quite a number of outstanding problems here awaiting solution.

The Party has always deemed it its duty to heighten the authority of the people's representatives, and, at the same time, to enhance their responsibility to the electorate in every way possible. The title of a deputy is not just something that goes with one's office; it is not an honorary privilege; it means a lot of hard work at the soviet and among the population. And we must do all we can for the strict observance of the law on the status of deputies, and see to it that every deputy should be afforded every opportunity to exercise his or her powers.

The development of the people's self-government calls for a further enhancement of democratic principles in administration, in the activity of soviets' executive committees, of their apparatus and of all other government bodies. Most of the people working in them are competent and take what they do close to heart. One should, however, always remember that, even if its executives are masterminds, no apparatus will ever get what it wants unless it relies on the working people's motivated support and participation in government. The times are increasingly exacting and rigid as regards the work of the apparatus. And there are quite a few shortcomings here; one often encounters a departmental approach and localism, irresponsibility, red tape and formal indifference to people. One of the main reasons for this is the slackening of control over the activity of the apparatus by the working people, the soviets themselves and the social organisations.

Bearing all this in mind, the Party has set itself the task of setting in motion all the instruments that actually enable every citizen to actively influence administrative decision-making, verify fulfilment of decisions, and get the requisite information about the activity of the apparatus. This purpose is to be served by a system of regular reports to work collectives and general meetings by all administrative bodies. Much can be done in this area by people's control committees, groups and teams, by voluntary trade union inspectors, and by the mass media.

The elective bodies themselves should be more exacting and strict towards their own apparatus. One cannot overlook the fact that executives who remain in office for long periods tend to lose their feel for the new, to shut themselves off from the people by instructions they have concocted themselves, and sometimes even hold back the work of elective bodies. It is obviously time to work out a procedure which would enable soviets, and all social bodies in general, to evaluate and certify the work of responsible executives of their apparatus after each election, making desirable personnel changes.

Ever more active involvement of social organisations in governing the country is needed in our time. When the work of our social organisations is considered from this angle, however, it becomes obvious that many of them are lacking in sufficient initiative. Some of them try to operate above all through their regular staff, in a bureaucratic way, and lean only a little on the masses. In other words, the popular, creative, independent nature of social organisations is not being fully realised by far.

In our country, the trade unions are the largest mass organisation. On the whole, they do a lot to satisfy the requirements of factory and office workers and collective farmers, to promote emulation, tighten discipline and heighten labour productivity. Still, trade union committees are in many cases lacking in militancy and resolve when defending the working people's legitimate interests, ensuring labour protection and safety, and constructing and running health-building, sports and cultural facilities. Understandably, such passivity suits those managers for whom production sometimes obscures the people. The trade unions, however, should always give priority to social policy, to promoting the working people's interests. Properly speaking, this is the basic purpose of their activity. The All-Union Central Council of Trade Unions and other trade union bodies enjoy extensive rights and control vast enough funds, both the state's and their own. It is up to them, therefore, to make wide and sure use of them, instead of waiting for somebody else to fulfil the tasks they are charged with.

Comrades, our future largely depends on the young people we are bringing up today. That is the task of the whole Party, of the whole people. It is the most important and basic task of the Leninist Young Communist League. The young people in our country are hard-working, ready for exploits and self-sacrifice, and devoted to socialism. Nonetheless, it is the duty of the older generations to do everything they can for those who will replace them to be still more intelligent, more capable and better educated, worthy of taking the baton and carrying into the future the ideals of justice and freedom bequeathed to us by the Great October Revolution.

As Lenin said, it is impossible to master communism through books alone, it is impossible to cultivate a sense of responsibility without charging people with responsible tasks. The young people of the 1980s are broad-minded, well-educated and vigorous. I should say, they are prepared for action and look for a chance to show their worth in all areas of public life. The YCL, too, must make every effort to support their drive in all areas—the national economy, science, engineering, in mastering knowledge and culture, in political life, and in defending the motherland. This effort, more than any other, should be of a questing nature, interesting and appealing to young people, and closely tied up with the needs of the young in production, study, home life and leisure.

Together with the YCL, the Party, government and economic bodies should consistently seek to promote deserving young people to high posts in management, production, science and culture. We say: in our country, all roads are open to young people. That is true. But persistent efforts are needed for these words not to lose lustre and the road for young people to be really wide.

By and large, the CPSU Central Committee deems it advisable to take further steps to increase the role of the trade unions, the YCL, the unions of creative workers and the voluntary societies in the system of the people's socialist self-government. In particular, it is planned to extend the range of questions which government bodies can settle only with the participation or prior agreement of trade unions, YCL or women's organisations and to grant these organisations the right to suspend, in some cases, the implementation of administrative decisions.

Our Party Programme aims at the most effective exercise of all forms of direct democracy, of direct participation by the popular masses in the elaboration, adoption and execution of governmental and other decisions. An enormous role is played here by the work collectives operating in all spheres of the life of society, and chiefly in the national economy. The granting of broader powers to enterprises, the introduction of cost accounting and promotion of the spirit of socialist enterprise will become truly effective only if the working man himself displays greater activity. We cannot put up with the still existing instances of workers not knowing the programmes of their own enterprise, of their suggestions not getting due attention and not being taken into account. These instances show that in some places the force of inertia determines the state of affairs, hinders the involvement of factory and office workers in management and impedes the process of fostering among them the feeling that they are full-fledged masters of production.

The law on work collectives adopted two years ago has indisputably stimulated initiatives by work collectives. But we cannot yet say this law is producing the results we expected. This is evident from the CPSU Central Committee's examination of the practice of applying it at the Minsk motor works and elsewhere. Our conclusion is unambiguous: it is necessary to radically improve the mechanism that enables us to make the democratic principles and norms of the law operative in everyday practice. Step by step we must extend the range of issues on which the work collective's decisions are final, enhance the role of the general meetings of factory and office workers and raise their responsibility for the implementation of their decisions. There has arisen the idea that a council, say, of the work collective, made up of representatives of the management, Party, trade union and YCL organisations, the team councils, rank-and-file workers and specialists, should function in the period between general meetings, both at the level of teams and the enterprise as a whole.

Today the advanced teams which apply the cost-accounting principle are already becoming primary self-government units that elect their managers. Life shows the viability of this practice. It has confirmed that in extending democratic economic management principles it appears advisable to spread the electivity principle to all team leaders and then gradually to some other categories of managerial personnel—foremen, shift, sector or shop superintendents, and state-farm department managers. Long years of experience testify that this is the direction in which we must look for modern forms of combining centralism and democracy, of combining one-man management and electivity, in running the national economy.

Undeviating observance of the democratic principles of guiding collective farms and other cooperative organisations, including observance of their rules, is a matter to which we pay constant attention. In recent times our efforts in this sphere have somehow relaxed, and too many organisations have been interfering in the activities of co-operative societies. Party and government bodies must see to it that collective-farm or co-operative self-government is exercised unfailingly, that any attempts to bring pressure to bear and to practice armchair management are thwarted.

Our Constitution provides for nation-wide discussions and referendums on major issues of our country's life and for discussions of decisions passed by local soviets. We must expedite the drafting of a law on this highly important question. We must make better use of such reliable channels for the development of direct democracy as meetings of citizens, constituents' mandates, people's letters, the press, radio, TV, as well as all other means of eliciting public opinion and of making a quick and attentive response to the people's needs and mood.

Broader publicity is a matter of principle to us. It is a political issue. Without publicity there is not, nor can there be, democracy, political creativity by the citizenry and participation by the citizenry in administration and management. If you like, this is an earnest of a responsible, statesmanlike attitude to the common cause on the part of millions upon millions of factory workers, collective farmers and intellectuals and a point of departure in the mental readjustment of our cadres.

When the subject of publicity comes up, calls are sometimes made for exercising greater caution when speaking about the shortcomings, omissions and difficulties that are inevitable in any ongoing effort. There can only be one answer to this, a Leninist answer: communists want the truth, always and under all circumstances. The experience of the past year has shown how forcefully Soviet people support an uncompromising appraisal of everything that impedes our advance. But those who have grown used to doing slipshod work, to practising deception, indeed feel really awkward in the glare of publicity, when everything done in the state and in society is under the people's control and is in full public view. Therefore, we must make publicity an unfailingly operative system. It is needed in the centre and no less, perhaps much more, in the localities, wherever people live and work. The citizen wants to know, and should know not only decisions taken on a country-wide scale but also decisions taken locally by Party and government bodies, factory managements and trade unions.

The whole range of the Soviet citizens' socio-political and personal rights and freedoms should promote the broadening and further development of socialist democracy. The Party and the state regard the deepening of these rights and freedoms and the strengthening of their guarantees as their primary duty. But the gist of socialism is that the rights of citizens do not, and cannot, exist outside their duties, just as there cannot be duties without corresponding rights.

It is essential to stimulate the activity of our citizens, of one and all, in constructive work, in eliminating shortcomings, abuses and all other unhealthy phenomena, all departures from our legal and moral standards. Democracy was and remains a major lever of strengthening socialist legality, and stable legality was and remains an inseparable part of our democracy.

A good deal of work has been done lately to strengthen law and order in all spheres of the life of society. But the efforts in this direction must not be slackened in any way. We must keep on improving soviet laws. Our legislation—the civil, labour, financial, administrative, economic and criminal laws—must help more vigorously in introducing economically viable management methods, in exercising effective control over the measure of labour and consumption and in translating the principles of social justice into reality.

We must persistently enhance the responsibility of the law-enforcement and other bodies, and strengthen the legal service in soviets and in the national economy, and state arbitration, and also improve the legal education of the population. As before, full use must be made of Soviet legislation in crime control and in combatting other breaches of the law, so that the people of all towns and villages can rest assured that the state concerns itself with their peace and inviolability, and that not a single wrongdoer evades the punishment deserved.

We must very strictly observe the democratic principles of justice, the equality of citizens before the law and other guarantees that protect the interests of the state and of every citizen. In this context it is necessary to take vigorous steps to upgrade the role of the procurators' supervision, to improve the functioning of courts of law and the bar, and to complete, in the near future, the drafting of a law, as provided for by the Constitution, on the procedure of filing appeals in court against unlawful actions by officials that infringe upon the rights of citizens. Naturally,

Mikhail Gorbachov and his wife, Raisa, upon arrival in Geneva for the summit in November 1985. General Secretary Gorbachov met with President Ronald Reagan to discuss arms control and other U.S.-Soviet issues.

the more vigorously the Party and government bodies, trade unions, the YCL, work collectives and volunteer public order squads, all the people, are involved in such effort, the more fully will legality and law and order be ensured.

In the context of the growing subversive activity by imperialist secret services against the Soviet Union and other socialist countries, greater responsibility devolves upon the state security bodies. Under the Party's leadership and scrupulously observing Soviet laws, these bodies are conducting extensive work to expose enemy intrigues, to frustrate all kinds of subversion and to protect our country's sacred frontiers. We are convinced that Soviet security forces and borderguards will always measure up to the demands made of them, will always display vigilance, self-control and tenacity in the struggle against any encroachment on our political social system.

Taking into account the complicated international situation and the growing aggressiveness of the reactionary imperialist quarters, the CPSU Central Committee and its Political Bureau pay unflagging attention to our country's defence capability, to the combat might of the armed forces of the USSR, to the tightening of military discipline. The Soviet Army and Navy possess modern arms and equipment, well-trained servicemen and skilled officers and political cadres, who are completely dedicated to the people. They acquit themselves with honour in the most complicated, and at times rigorous, situations. Today we can declare with all responsibility that the defence capability of the USSR is maintained at a level that reliably protects the peaceful life and labour of the Soviet people.

The Party and the government have always striven to ensure that the Soviet soldier and officer unfailingly receive our society's care and attention while performing their arduous duties, and that our armed forces are a school of civil responsibility, fortitude and patriotism.

It is clear, comrades, that here, at this Congress, we are merely outlining the general frameworks and the main contours of perfecting our democracy, statehood, and the entire Soviet political system. Implementation of the Congress decisions will undoubtedly bring to light fresh manifestations of the people's initiative and new forms of mass socio-political creativity.

IV. BASIC ARMS AND DIRECTIONS OF THE PARTY'S FOREIGN POLICY STRATEGY

The tasks underlying the country's economic and social development also determine the CPSU's strategy on the world scene. Its main aim is crystal clear—to ensure to the Soviet people the possibility of working under conditions of enduring peace and freedom. Such, in essence, is the Party's primary programme requirement of our foreign policy. To fulfil it in the present situation means, above all, to terminate the material preparations for a nuclear war.

After having weighed all the aspects of the situation that has taken shape, the CPSU has put forward a coherent programme for the total abolition of weapons of mass destruction before the end of this century, a programme that is historic in terms of its dimensions and significance. Its realisation would open for mankind a fundamentally new period of development and the opportunity to concentrate entirely on constructive labour.

As you know, we have addressed our proposals not only through the traditional diplomatic channels but also directly to world public opinion, to the peoples. The time has come to have a thorough understanding of the harsh realities of our day: nuclear weapons harbour a hurricane with the potential of sweeping the human race from the face of the Earth. Our address further underscores the open, honest, Leninist character of the CPSU's foreign policy strategy.

Socialism unconditionally rejects war as a means of settling state-to-state political and economic contradictions and ideological disputes. Our ideal is a world without weapons and violence, a world in which each people freely chooses its path of development, its way of life. This is an expression of the humanism of communist ideology, of its moral values. That is why for the future as well the struggle against the nuclear menace, against the arms race, for the preservation and strengthening of universal peace remains the fundamental direction of the Party's activities on the international scene.

There is no alternative to this policy. This is all the more true in periods of tension in international affairs. I would say that never in the decades since the war has the situation in the world been so explosive, and consequently complex and uncongenial as in the first half of the 1980s. The right-wing group that came to power in the USA and its main NATO fellow-travellers made a steep turn from detente to a policy of military force. They have adopted doctrines that reject good-neighbourly relations and co-operation as a principle of world development, as a political philosophy of international relations. The administration in Washington remained deaf to our calls for an end to the arms race and an improvement of the situation.

Perhaps it may not be worth churning up the past? Especially today when in Soviet-US relations there seem to be signs of a change for the better, and realistic trends are beginning to resurface in the actions and attitudes of the leadership of some NATO nations. We feel that it is worthwhile, for the drastic frosting of the international climate in the first half of the 1980s was a further reminder that nothing comes of itself: peace has to be fought for, and this has to be a persevering and meaningful fight. We have to look for, find, and use even the smallest opportunity in order—while this is still possible—to halt the trend towards an escalation of the threat of war. Appreciating this, the Central Committee of the CPSU at its plenary meeting once again analysed the character and dimensions of the nuclear threat and defined the practical steps that could lead to an improvement of the situation. We were guided by the following considerations of principle.

First. The character of present-day weaponry leaves no country with any hope of safeguarding itself solely with military and technical means, for example by building up a defence, even the most powerful. To ensure security is increasingly seen as a political problem, and it can only be resolved by political means. In order to progress along the road of disarmament what is needed is, above all, the will. Security cannot be built endlessly on fear of retaliation, in other words, on the doctrines of 'containment' or 'deterrence'. Apart from the absurdity and amorality of a situation in which the whole world becomes a nuclear hostage, these doctrines encourage an arms race that may sooner or later go out of control.

Second. In the context of the relations between the USSR and the USA, security can only be mutual, and if we take international relations as a whole it can only be universal. The highest wisdom is not in caring exclusively for oneself, especially to the detriment of the other side. It is vital that all should feel equally secure, for the fears and anxieties of the nuclear age generate uncertainty in politics and concrete actions. It is becoming extremely important to take the critical significance of the time factor into account. The appearance of new systems of weapons of mass destruction steadily shortens time and narrows down the possibilities for adopting political decisions on questions of war and peace in crisis situations.

Third. The USA, its military-industrial machine remains the locomotive of militarism, for so far it has no intention of slowing down. This has to be taken into consideration, of course. But we are well aware that the interests and aims of the military-industrial complex are not at all the same as the interests and aims of the American people, as the actual national interests of that great country.

Naturally, the world is much larger than the USA and its occupation bases on foreign soil. And in world politics one cannot confine oneself to relations with any single, even a very important, country. As we know from experience, this only fosters the arrogance of strength. Needless to say, we attach considerable significance to the state and character of the relations between the Soviet Union and the USA. Our countries have quite a few points of coincidence, and there is the objective need to live in peace with each other, to co-operate on a basis of equality and mutual benefit, and there is no other basis.

Fourth. The world is in a process of swift changes, and it is not within anybody's power to maintain a perpetual status quo in it. It consists in many scores of countries, each having interests that are perfectly legitimate. All without exception face a task of fundamental significance: without being blind to social, political, and ideological differences all have to master the science and art of restraint and circumspection on the international scene, to live in a civilised manner, in other words, under conditions of civil international intercourse and co-operation. But to give this co-operation wide scope there has to be an all-embracing system of international economic security that would in equal measure protect every nation against discrimination, sanctions and other attributes of imperialist, neocolonialist policy. Alongside disarmament such a system can become a dependable pillar of international security generally.

In short, the modern world has become much too small and fragile for wars and a policy of force. It cannot be saved and preserved if the thinking and actions built up over the centuries on the acceptability and permissibility of wars and armed conflicts are not shed once and for all, irrevocably.

This means the realisation that it is no longer possible to win an arms race, or nuclear war for that matter. The continuation of this race on Earth, let alone its spread to outer space, will accelerate the already critically high rate of stockpiling and perfecting nuclear weapons. The situation in the world may become such that it will no longer depend upon the intelligence or will of political leaders. It may become captive to technology, to technocratic military logic. Consequently, not only nuclear war itself but also the preparations for it, in other words the arms race and the aspiration to win military superiority, can—speaking in objective terms—bring no political gain to anybody.

Further, this means understanding that the present level of the balance of the nuclear capabilities of the opposite sides is much too high. For the time being this ensures equal danger to each of them. But only for the time being. Continuation of the nuclear arms race will inevitably heighten this equal threat and may bring it to a point where even parity will cease to be a factor of military-political deterrence. Consequently it is vital, in the first place, to dramatically reduce the level of military confrontation. In our age, genuine equal security is guaranteed not by an excessively high but by the lowest possible level of strategic parity, from which nuclear and other types of weapons of mass destruction must be totally excluded.

Lastly, this means realising that in the present situation there is no alternative to co-operation and interaction between all countries. Thus, the objective—I emphasise, objective—conditions have taken shape in which confrontation between capitalism and socialism can proceed only and exclusively in forms of peaceful competition and peaceful contest.

For us peaceful coexistence is a political course which the USSR intends to go on following unswervingly. In ensuring the continuity of its foreign policy strategy, the CPSU will pursue a vigorous international policy stemming from the realities of the world we live in. Of course, the problem of international security cannot be resolved by one or two, even very intensive, peace offensives. Success can only be brought by consistent, methodical and persevering effort.

Continuity in foreign policy has nothing in common with a simple repetition of what has been done, especially in tackling the problems that have piled up. What is wanted is a high degree of accuracy in assessing one's own possibilities, restraint, and an eminently high sense of responsibility when decisions are made. What is wanted is firmness in upholding principles and postures, tactical flexibility, a readiness for mutually acceptable compromises, and an orientation on dialogue and mutual understanding rather than on confrontation.

As you know, we have made a series of unilateral steps—we put a moratorium on the deployment of intermediate-range missiles in Europe, cut back the number of these missiles, and stopped all nuclear tests. In Moscow and abroad there have been talks with leaders and members of the governments of many countries. The Soviet-Indian, Soviet-French, and Soviet-U.S. summits were necessary and useful steps.

The Soviet Union has made energetic efforts to give a fresh impetus to the negotiations in Geneva, Stockholm and Vienna, the purpose of which is to scale down the arms race and build up confidence between states. Negotiations are always a delicate and complex matter. Of cardinal importance here is to lead up to a mutually acceptable balance of interests. To turn weapons of mass destruction into an object of political scheming is, to say the least, immoral, while in political terms this is irresponsible.

Lastly, concerning our statement of January 15 of this year. Taken as a whole, our programme is essentially an alloy of the philosophy of shaping a safe world in the nuclear-space age with a platform of concrete actions. The Soviet Union offers approaching the problems of disarmament in their totality, for in terms of security they are linked with one another. I am not speaking of rigid linkages or attempts at 'backing down' in one direction in order to erect barricades in another. What I am talking about is a plan of concrete actions strictly measured out in terms of time. The USSR intends to work perseveringly for its realisation, regarding it as the central direction for our foreign policy for the coming years.

The Soviet military doctrine is also entirely in keeping with the letter and spirit of the initiatives we have put forward. Its orientation is unequivocally defensive. In the military sphere we intend to act in such a way as to give nobody grounds for fears, even imagined, about their security. But to an equal extent we and our allies want to be rid of the feeling that we are threatened. The USSR undertook the obligation not to be the first to use nuclear weapons and it will abide strictly by that obligation. But it is no secret that scenarios for a nuclear strike against us exist. We have no right to overlook this. The Soviet Union is a staunch adversary of nuclear war in any variant. Our country stands for removing weapons of mass destruction from use, for limiting the military potential to reasonable adequacy. But the character and level of this ceiling continues to be limited by the attitudes and actions of the USA and its bloc partners. Under these conditions we repeat again and again: the Soviet Union lays no claim to more security, but it will not settle for less.

I should like to draw attention to the problem of verification, to which we attach special significance. We have declared on several occasions that the USSR is open to verification, that we are interested in it as much as anybody else. All-embracing, strictest verification is perhaps the key element of the disarmament process. The essence of the matter, in our thinking, is that there can be no disarmament without verification and that verification without disarmament makes no sense.

There is yet another matter of principle. We have stated our attitude to 'Star Wars' quite substantively. The USA has already drawn many of its allies into this programme. There is the danger that things may become irreversible. Before it is too late, it is imperative to find a realistic solution guaranteeing that the arms race does not spread to outer space. The 'Star Wars' programme cannot be permitted to be used as stimulus for a further arms race or as a road-block to radical disarmament. Tangible progress in what concerns a drastic reduction of nuclear capabilities can be of much help to surmount this obstacle. For that reason the Soviet Union is prepared to make a substantial step in that direction, to resolve the question of intermediate-range missiles in the European zone separately—without a direct link to problems related to strategic armaments and outer space.

The Soviet programme has touched the hearts of millions of people, and among political leaders and public personalities interest in it continues to grow. The times today are such that it is hard to brush it off. The attempts to sow doubt about the Soviet Union's constructive commitment to accelerate, to tackle this pressing problem of our day—the destruction of nuclear weapons—in practical terms are becoming less and less convincing. Nuclear disarmament should not be the exclusive domain of political leaders. The whole world is now pondering this, for it is a question of life itself.

But, also it is necessary to take into account the reaction of the centres of power that hold in their hands the keys to the success or failure of disarmament. Of course, the U.S. ruling class, to be more exact its most egotistical groups linked to the military-industrial complex, have other aims that are clearly antipodal to ours. For them disarmament spells out a loss of profits and a political risk, for us it is a blessing in all respects—economically, politically and morally.

We know our principal opponents and have accumulated a complex and extensive experience in our relations and talks with them. The day before yesterday, we received President Reagan's reply to our statement of January 15. The U.S. side began to set forth its considerations in greater detail at the talks in Geneva. To be sure, we shall closely examine everything the U.S. side has to say on these matters. However, since the reply was received literally on the eve of the Congress, the U.S. Administration apparently expects, as we see it, our attitude to the U.S. stand to be made known to the world from this rostrum.

What I can say right away is that the President's letter does not give ground for amending the assessment of the international situation as had been set forth in the report before the reply was received. It says that the elimination of nuclear arms is the goal all the nuclear powers should strive after. In his letter the President agrees in general with some or other Soviet proposals and intentions as regards the issues of disarmament and security. In other words, the reply seems to contain some reassuring opinions and theses.

However, these positive pronouncements are swamped in various reservations, 'linkages' and 'conditions' which in fact block the solution of radical problems of disarmament. Reduction in the strategic nuclear arsenals is made conditional on our consent to the 'Star Wars' programme and reductions, unilateral, by the way, in the Soviet conventional arms. Linked to this are also problems of regional conflicts and bilateral relations. The elimination of nuclear arms in Europe is blocked by the references to the stand taken by Great Britain and France and the demand to weaken our defences in the eastern part of the country, with the U.S. military forces retained as they are. The refusal to stop nuclear tests is justified by arguments to the effect that nuclear weapons serve as a factor of "containment". This is in direct contradiction with the purpose reaffirmed in the letter—the need to destroy nuclear weapons. The reluctance of the USA and its ruling circles to embark on the path of nuclear disarmament manifests itself most clearly in their attitude to nuclear explosions, the termination of which is the demand of the whole world.

To put it in a nutshell, it is hard to detect in the letter we have just received any serious preparedness of the U.S. Administration to get down to solving the cardinal problems involved in eliminating the nuclear threat. It looks as if some people in Washington and elsewhere, for that matter, have got used to living side by side with nuclear weapons linking with them their plans in the international arena. However, whether they want it or not, the Western politicians will have to answer the question: are they prepared to part with nuclear weapons at all?

In accordance with an understanding reached in Geneva there will be another meeting with the U.S. President. The significance that we attach to it is that it ought to produce practical results in key areas of limiting and reducing armaments. There are at least two matters on which an understanding could be reached: the cessation of nuclear tests and the abolition of U.S. and Soviet intermediate-range missiles in the European zone. And then, as a matter of fact, if there is readiness to seek agreement, the question of the time of the meeting would be resolved of itself: we will accept any suggestion on this count. But there is no sense in holding empty talks. We shall not remain indifferent if the Soviet-U.S. dialogue that has started and inspired some not unfounded hopes of a possibility for changes for the better is used to continue the arms race and the material preparations for war. The Soviet Union is of a firm mind to justify the hopes of the peoples of our two countries and of the whole world who are expecting concrete steps, practical actions and tangible agreements of the leaders of the USSR and the USA on how to block the arms race. We are prepared for this.

Naturally, like any other country, we attach considerable importance to the security of our frontiers, on land and at sea. We have many neighbours, and they are different. We have no territorial claims on any of them. We threaten none of them. But as experience has shown time and again, there are quite a few persons who, in disregard of the national interests of either our country or those of countries neighbouring upon us, are endeavouring to aggravate the situation on the frontiers of the Soviet Union.

For instance, counter-revolution and imperialism have turned Afghanistan into a bleeding wound. The USSR supports that country's efforts to defend its sovereignty. We should like, in the nearest future, to withdraw the Soviet troops stationed in Afghanistan at the request of its government. Moreover, we have agreed with the Afghan side on the schedule for their phased withdrawal as soon as a political settlement is reached that ensures an actual cessation and dependably guarantees the non-resumption of foreign armed interference in the internal affairs of the Democratic Republic of Afghanistan. It is in our vital, national interest that the USSR should always have good and peaceful relations with all its neighbours. This is a vitally important objective of our foreign policy.

The CPSU regards the European direction as one of the main directions of its international activity. Europe's historic opportunity and its future lie in peaceful co-operation among the nations of that continent. And it is important, while preserving the assets that have already been accumulated, to move further; from the initial to a more lasting phase of detente, to mature detente, and then to the building of dependable security on the basis of the Helsinki process, of a radical reduction of nuclear and conventional weapons.

The significance of the Asian and Pacific direction is growing. In that vast region there are many tangled knots of contradictions and, besides, the political situation in some places is unstable. Here it is necessary, without postponement, to find the relevant solutions and paths. Evidently, this has to begin with the coordination and then the pooling of efforts in the interests of a political settlement of painful problems so as, in parallel, on that basis to at least take the edge off the military confrontation in various parts of Asia and stabilise the situation there.

Andrei Gromyko, President of the Supreme Soviet Presidium, Mikhail Gorbachov, General Secretary, and Nikolai Tikonov, Chairman of the Council of Ministers, at the Bolshoi Theater International Women's Day Gala on March 7, 1985.

This is made all the more urgent by the fact that in Asia and other continents the flashpoints of military danger are not dying down. We are in favour of vitalising collective quests for ways of defusing conflict situations in the Middle East, Central America, South Africa, in all of the planet's turbulent points. This is imperatively demanded by the interests of general security.

Crises and conflicts are fertile soil also for international terrorism. Undeclared wars, the export of counter-revolution in all forms, political assassination, the taking of hostages, the hijacking of aircraft, and bomb attacks in streets, at airports and railway stations—such is the hideous face of terrorism, which its instigators try to mask with various cynical inventions. The USSR rejects terrorism in principle and is prepared to co-operate actively with other states in order to uproot it. The Soviet union will resolutely safeguard its citizens against acts of violence and do everything to defend their lives, honour and dignity.

Looking back over the past year one will see that, by all the evidence, the prerequisites for improving the international situation are beginning to form. But prerequisites for a turn are not the turn itself. The arms race continues and the threat of nuclear war remains. However, international reaction is by no means omnipotent. The development of the world revolutionary process and the growth of mass democratic and anti-war movements have significantly enlarged and strengthened the huge potential of peace, reason and good will. This is a powerful counter-balance to imperialism's aggressive policy.

The destinies of peace and social progress are now linked more closely than ever before with the dynamic character of the socialist world system's economic and political development. The need for this dynamism is dictated by concern for the welfare of the peoples. But for the socialist world it is necessary also from the standpoint of counteraction to the military threat. Lastly, in this lies a demonstration of the potentialities of the socialist way of life. We are watched by both friends and foes. We are watched by the huge and heterogeneous world of developing nations. It is looking for its choice, for its road, and what this choice is will depend to a large extent on socialism's successes, on the credibility of its answers to the challenges of time.

We are convinced that socialism can resolve the most difficult problems confronting it. Of vital significance for this is the increasingly vigorous interaction whose effect is not merely the adding up but the multiplication of our potentials and which serves as a stimulus for common advancement. This is mirrored also in joint documents of countries of the socialist community.

Interaction between governing communist parties remains the heart and soul of the political co-operation among these countries. During the past year there has practically been no fraternal countries with whose leaders we have not had meetings and detailed talks. The forms of such co-operation are themselves being updated. A new and perhaps key element, the multilateral working meetings of leaders of fraternal countries, is being institutionalised. These allow for prompt and friendly consultations on the entire spectrum of problems of socialist construction, on its internal and external aspects.

In the difficult international situation the prolongation of the Warsaw Treaty by a unanimous decision of its signatories was of great significance. This treaty saw its second birth, so to speak, and today it is hard to picture world politics as a whole without it. Take the Sofia Conference of the treaty's Political Consultative Committee. It was a kind of threshold of the Geneva dialogue.

In the economic sphere there is now the comprehensive programme of scientific and technological progress. Its import lies in the transition of the CMEA countries to a coordinated policy in science and technology. The accent is being shifted from primarily commercial relations to specialisation and co-operation of production, particularly in heavy engineering. In our view, changes are also required in the work of the headquarters of socialist integration—the Council for Mutual Economic Assistance. But the main thing is that in carrying out this programme there is less armchair administration and fewer committees and commissions of all sorts, that more attention is given to economic levers, initiative and socialist enterprise, and that work collectives are drawn into this process. This would indeed be a committed approach to such an extraordinary undertaking.

Vitality, efficiency and initiative—all these qualities meet the imperatives of the times, and we shall strive to have them spread throughout the system of relations between fraternal parties. The CPSU attaches growing significance to live and broad communication between citizens of socialist countries, between people of different professions and different generations. This is a source of mutual intellectual enrichment, a channel for exchanges of views, ideas and the experience of socialist construction. Today it is especially important to analyse the character of the socialist way of life and understand the processes of perfecting democracy, management methods and personnel policy on the basis of the development of several countries rather than of one country. A considerate and respectful attitude to each other's experience and the employment of this experience in practice are a huge potential of the socialist world.

Generally speaking, one of socialism's advantages is its ability to learn: to learn to resolve the problems posed by life; to learn to forestall the crisis situations that our class adversary tries to create and utilise; to learn to counter the attempts to divide the socialist world and play off some countries against others; to learn to prevent collisions of the interests of different socialist countries, harmonise them by mutual effort, and find mutually acceptable solutions even to the most intricate problems.

It seems to us that it is worth taking a close look also at the relations in the socialist world as a whole. We do not see the community as being separated by some barrier from other socialist countries. The CPSU stands for honest, above-board relations with all communist parties and all countries of the socialist world system, for comradely exchanges of opinion between them. Above all, we endeavour to see what unites the socialist world. For that reason the Soviet Communists are gladdened by every step towards closer relations among all socialist states, by every positive advance in these relations.

One can say with gratification that there has been a measure of improvement of the Soviet Union's relations with its great neighbour—socialist China. The distinctions in attitudes, in particular, to a number of international problems remain. But we also note something else—that in many cases we can work jointly, co-operate on an equal and principled basis, without prejudice to third countries.

There is no need to explain the significance of this. The Chinese Communists called the victory of the USSR and the forces of progress in the Second World War a prologue to the triumph of the People's Revolution in China. In turn, the formation of People's China helped to reinforce socialism's positions in the world and disrupt many of imperialism's designs and actions in the difficult postwar years. In thinking of the future, it may be said that the potentialities for co-operation between the USSR and China are enormous. They are great because such co-operation is in line with the interests of both countries; because what is dearest to our peoples—socialism and peace—is indivisible.

The CPSU is an inalienable component of the international communist movement. We, the Soviet Communists, are well aware that every advance we make in building socialism is an advance of the entire movement. For that reason the CPSU sees its primary internationalist duty in ensuring our country's successful progress along the road opened and blazed by the October Revolution.

The communist movement in the non-socialist part of the world remains the principal target of political pressure and harassment by reactionary circles of the bourgeoisie. All the fraternal parties are constantly under fire from anti-communist propaganda, which does not hold back from the most despicable means and methods. Many parties operate underground, in a situation of unmitigated persecution and repression. Every step the communists take calls for struggle and personal courage. Permit me, comrades, on behalf of the 27th Congress, on behalf of the Soviet Communists to express sincere admiration for the dedicated struggle of our comrades, and profound fraternal solidarity with them.

In recent years the communist movement has come face to face with many new realities, tasks and problems. All the indications are that it has entered upon a qualitatively new phase of development. The international conditions of the work of communists are changing rapidly and profoundly. A substantial restructuring is taking place in the social pattern of bourgeois society, including the composition of the working class. The problems arising for our friends in the new independent states are not simple. The scientific and technological revolution is exercising a contradictory influence on the material conditions and consciousness of working people in the non-socialist world. All this requires the ability to do a lot of rethinking and demands a bold and creative approach to the new realities on the basis of the immortal theory of Marx, Engels and Lenin. The CPSU knows this well from its own experience.

The communist movement's immense diversity and the tasks that it encounters are likewise a reality. In some cases this leads to disagreements and divergences. The CPSU is not dramatising the fact that complete unanimity among communist parties exists not always and not in everything. Evidently, there generally cannot be an identity of views on all issues without exception. The communist movement came into being when the working class entered the international scene as an independent and powerful political force. The parties that comprise it have grown on national soil and pursue a common end objective—peace and socialism. Precisely this is the main, determining thing that unites them.

We do not see the diversity of our movement as a synonym for disunity, much as unity has nothing in common with uniformity, hierarchy, interference by some parties in the affairs of others, or the striving for any party to have a monopoly over what is right. The communist movement can and should be strong by virtue of its class solidarity, of equal co-operation among all the fraternal parties in the struggle for common aims. This is how the CPSU understands unity and intends to do everything to foster it.

The trend towards strengthening the potential of peace, reason and good will is enduring and in principle irreversible. At the back of it is the aspiration of people, of all nations to live on concord and to co-operate. However, one should look at things realistically: the balance of strength in the struggle against war is shaping in the course of an acute and dynamic confrontation between progress and reaction. An immutable factor is the CPSU's solidarity with the forces of national liberation and social emancipation, and our course towards close interaction with socialist-oriented countries, with revolutionary-democratic parties and with the Non-Aligned Movement. The Soviet public is prepared to go on promoting links with non-communist movements and organisations, including religious organisations militating against war.

This is also the angle from which the CPSU regards its relations with the social democratic movement. It is a fact that the idelogical differences between the communists and the social democrats are deep, and that their achievements and experience are dissimilar and non-equivalent. However, an unbiased look at the standpoints and views of each other is unquestionably useful to both the communists and the social democrats, useful in the first place for furthering the struggle for peace and international security.

We are living in a world of realities and are building our international policy in keeping with the specific features of the present phase of international developments. Our creative analysis of this phase and vision of prospects have led us to a conclusion that is highly significant. As never before it is now important to find ways for closer and more productive co-operation with governments, parties and mass organisations and movements that are in fact preoccupied with the destinies of peace on Earth, with all peoples in order to build an all-embracing system of international security.

We see the fundamental principles of this system in the following:

1. IN THE MILITARY SPHERE

—renunciation by the nuclear powers of war—both nuclear and conventional—against each other or against third countries;

—prevention of an arms race in outer space, cessation of all nuclear weapons, a ban on and the destruction of chemical weapons, and renunciation of the development of other means of mass annihilation;

—a strictly controlled lowering of the levels of military capabilities of countries to limits of reasonable adequacy;

—disbandment of military alliances, and as a stage towards this—renunciation of their enlargement and the formation of new ones;

—balanced and commensurate reduction of military budgets.

2. IN THE POLITICAL SPHERE

—unconditional respect in international practice for the right of each people to choose the ways and forms of its development independently;

—a just political settlement of international crises and regional conflicts;

—elaboration of a set of measures aimed at building confidence between states and the creation f effective guarantees against attack from without and of the inviolability of their frontiers;

—elaboration of effective methods of preventing international terrorism, including the safety of nternational land, air and sea communications.

. IN THE ECONOMIC SPHERE

—exclusion of all forms of discrimination from international practice; renunciation of the policy f economic blockades and sanctions if this is not directly envisaged in the recommendations of he world community;

—joint quest for ways for a just settlement of the problem of debts;

—establishment of a new world economic order guaranteeing equal economic security to all ountries;

—elaboration of principles for utilising part of the funds released as a result of a reduction of nilitary budgets for the good of the world community, of developing nations in the first place;

—the pooling of efforts in exploring and making peaceful use of outer space and in resolving lobal problems on which the destinies of civilisation depend.

. IN THE HUMANITARIAN SPHERE

—co-operation in the dissemination of the ideas of peace, disarmament and international security; greater flow of general objective information and intercourse between peoples for the purpose f learning about one another; reinforcement of the spirit of mutual understanding and concord n the relations between them;

—extirpation of genocide, apartheid, advocacy of fascism and every other form of racial, national r religious exclusiveness, and also of discrimination against people on this basis;

—extension—while respecting the laws of each country—of international co-operation in the mplementation of the political, social and personal rights of people;

—decision in a humane and positive spirit of questions related to the reuniting of families, mariage, and the promotion of contacts between people and between organisations;

—strengthening of and quests for new forms of co-operation in culture, art, science, education nd medicine.

These principles stem logically from the provisions of the Programme of the CPSU. They are ntirely in keeping with our concrete foreign policy intiatives. Guided by them it would be possible to make peaceful coexistence the highest principle of state-to-state relations. In our view, hese principles could become the point of departure and a sort of guideline for a direct and systematic dialogue between leaders of countries of the world community—both bilateral and nultilateral.

And since this concerns the destinies of peace, such a dialogue is particularly important among he permanent members of the Security Council—the five nuclear powers. They bear the main urden of responsibility for the destinies of humankind. I emphasise—not a privilege, not a foundation for claims to 'leadership' in world affairs, but responsibility, about which nobody has the ight to forget. Why then should their leaders not gather at a round table and discuss what could nd should be done to strengthen peace?

As we see it, the entire existing mechanism of arms limitation negotiations should also start o function at top productivity. Can one 'grow accustomed' to the fact that for years these talks ave been proceeding on a parallel course, so to speak, with a simultaneous build-up of rmaments?

The USSR is giving considerable attention to a joint examination of the world economy's roblems, and prospects, the interdependence between disarmament and development, and the xpansion of trade and scientific and technological co-operation at international forums, as well s within the framework of the Helsinki process. We feel that in the future it would be important o convene a world congress on problems of economic security at which it would be possible to iscuss in a package everything that encumbers world economic relations.

We are prepared to consider seriously any other proposal aimed at the same direction.

Under all circumstances success must be achieved in the battle to prevent war. This would be n epoch-making victory of the whole of humanity, of every person on Earth. The CPSU sees ctive participation in this battle as the essence of its foreign policy strategy.

V. THE PARTY

The magnitude and novelty of what we have to do make exceptionally high demands of the char acter, of the political, ideological and organisational work conducted by the CPSU, which toda has more than 19 million members welded together by unity of purpose, will and discipline.

The Party's strength is that it has a feel for time, that it feels the beat of the pulse of life, an always works among the people. Whenever the country faces new problems the Party finds way of resolving them, restructures and remoulds leadership methods, demonstrating its ability t measure up to its historic responsibility for the country's destiny, for the cause of socialism an communism.

Life constantly verifies our potentialities. Last year was special in this respect. As never befor there was a need for unity in the Party ranks and unity in the Central Committee. We saw clearl that it was no longer possible to evade pressing issues of society's development, to remain recon ciled to irresponsibility, laxity and inertness. Under these conditions the Political Bureau, th Central Committee Secretariat and the Central Committee decided that the cardinal issues dic tated by the times had to be resolved. An important landmark on this road was the April plenar meeting of the Central Committee. We told the people frankly about the difficulties and omis sions in our work and about the plans for the immediate future and the long term. Today, at th Congress, we can state with confidence that the course set by the April plenary meeting receive the active support of the Communists, of millions of working people.

The present stage, which is one of society's qualitative transformation, requires the Party an each of its organisations to make new efforts, to be principled in assessing their own work, an show efficiency and dedication. The draft new edition of the Party Programme and the draf amendments in the Rules of the CPSU presented to the Congress proceed from the premise tha the task of mobilising all the factors of acceleration can only be carried out by a Party that ha the interest of the people at heart, a Party having a scientifically substantiated perspective, assert ing by its labour the confidence that the set targets would be attained.

The Party can resolve new problems successfully if it is itself in uninterrupted developmen free of the 'infallibility' complex, critically assesses the results that have been attained, an clearly sees what has to be done. The new requirements being made of cadres, of the entire style methods and character of work are dictated by the magnitude and complexity of the problem and the need to draw lessons from the past without compromise or reservations.

At the present, comrades, we have to focus on the practical organisation of our work and th placing and upbringing of cadres, of the body of Party activists, and reconsider our entire wor with a fresh Party view—at all levels, in all echelons. In this context, I should like to remin you of Lenin's words: "when the situation has changed and different problems have to be solved we cannot look back and attempt to solve them by yesterday's methods. Don't try—you won' succeed!" *(Collected Works,* Vol. 33, p. 173.)

1. WORK IN A NEW WAY, ENHANCE THE ROLE AND RESPONSIBILITY O PARTY ORGANISATIONS

The purpose of restructuring Party work is that each Party organisation—from republican to pri mary—should vigorously implement the course set by the April plenary meeting and live in a atmosphere of quest, of renewal of the forms and methods of its activity. This can only be don through the efforts of all the communists, the utmost promotion of democracy within the Part itself, the application of the principle of collective leadership at all levels, the promotion of criti cism and self-criticism, control and a responsible attitude to the work at hand. It is only the that the spirit of novelty is generated, that inertness and stagnation become intolerable.

We are justifiably exasperated by all sorts of shortcomings and by those responsible for them— people who neglect their duties and are indifferent to society's interests: hackworker and idler grabber and writer of anonymous letters, petty bureaucrat and bribe-taker. But they live and wor in a concrete collective, town or village, in a given organisation rather than some place awa from us. Then who save the collective and the communists should candidly declare that in ou working society each person is obliged to work conscientiously and abide strictly by the norms c socialist human association, which are the same for everybody. What and who prevent this?

This is where the task of enhancing the role of the Party organisation rises to its full stature

It does not become us, the communists, to put the blame on anybody. If a Party organisation lives a full-blooded life founded on relations of principle, if communists are engaged in concrete matters and not in a talking-shop on general subjects, success is assured. It is not enough to see shortcomings and defects, to stigmatise them. It is necessary to do everything so that they should not exist. There is no vanguard role of the communists generally; it is expressed in practical deeds.

Party life that is healthy, business-like, multiform in its concrete manifestations and concerns, characterised by openness and publicity of plans and decisions, by the humaneness and modesty of communists—that is what we need today. We, the communists, are looked upon as an example in everything—in work and behaviour. We have to live and work in such a way that the working person could say: "Yes, this is a real communist." And the more radiant and cleaner life will be in the Party house, the sooner will we cope with problems which are not simple and are typical of the present time of change.

Guided by the decisions of the April and subsequent Central Committee plenary meetings and working boldly and perseveringly, many Party organisations have achieved good results. In defining the ways for advancement, the CPSU Central Committee relies chiefly on that experience, striving to make it common property. For example, the decisions on accelerating scientific and technological progress are based to a large extent on the innovatory approach to these matters in the Leningrad Party organisation, and its experience underlies the drafting of the programmes for the intensification and integration of science and production, and socio-economic planning. Party organisations in the Ukraine should be commended for creating scientific and technological complexes and engineering centres and for their productive work in effectively utilising recycled resources. The measures to form a unified agro-industrial complex in the country underwent a preliminary trial in Georgia and Estonia.

Many examples could be given of a modern approach to work. A feel for the new and active restructuring in accordance with the changing conditions are a characteristic of the Byelorussian, Latvian, Sverdlovsk, Chelyabinsk, Krasnodar, Omsk, Ulyanovsk and other organisations. Evidence of this is also provided by many election meetings, conferences and republican congresses. They were notable for their business-like formulation of issues, the commitment of communists to seeking untapped resources and ways of speeding up our progress, and exactingness in assessing the work of elective bodies.

But the need for restructuring is seen by far from everybody and far from everywhere. There still are many organisations, as is likewise confirmed by the election campaign, in which one does not feel the proper frame of mind for a serious, self-critical analysis, for drawing practical conclusions. This is the effect of adherence to the old, the absence of a feel for the time, a propensity for excessive organisation, the habit of speaking vaguely, and the fear of revealing the real state of affairs.

We will not move forward a single step if we do not learn to work in a new way, do not put an end to inertness and conservatism in any of their forms, if we lose the courage to assess the situation realistically and see it as it actually is. To make irresponsibility recede into the past, we have to make a rule of calling things by their names, of judging everything openly. It is about time to stop exercises in misplaced tact where there should be exactingness and honesty, a Party conscience. Nobody has the right to forget Lenin's stern warning: "False rhetoric and false boastfulness spell moral ruin and lead unfailingly to political extinction." *(Collected Works, Vol. 9 p. 297.)*

The consistent implementation of the principle of collectivity is a key condition for a healthy life in every Party organisation. But in some organisations the role of plenary meetings and of the bureaus as collegiate bodies was downgraded, and the joint drafting of decisions was replaced by instructions issued by one individual, and this often led to gross errors. Such side-tracking of the norms of Party life was tolerated in the Central Committee of the Communist Party of Kirghizia. A principled assessment was given at the Congress of the Republic's Communist Party of the activities not only of the former First Secretary but also of those who connived at unscrupulousness and servility.

It is only strict compliance with and the utmost strengthening of the principle of collective leadership that can be a barrier to subjectivist kinks and create the conditions for the adoption of considered and substantial decisions. A leader who understands this clearly has the right to count on long and productive work.

More urgently than before there is now the need to promote criticism and self-criticism and step up the efforts to remove window-dressing. From the recent past we know that where criticism and self-criticism chokes, where talk about successes is substituted for a Party analysis of the actual situation, all Party activity is deformed and a situation of complacency, permissiveness and impunity arises that leads to the most serious consequencies. In the localities and even in the centre there appeared quite a few officials who reacted painfully to critical remarks levelled at them and went so far as to harass people who came up with criticism.

The labour achievements of the people of Moscow are widely known. But one can say confidently that these accomplishments would have been much greater had the City Party organisation not since some time ago lost the spirit of self-criticism and a healthy dissatisfaction with what had been achieved, and had complacency not surfaced. As was noted at a City Party Conference, the leadership of the City Committee had evaded decisions on complex problems while parading its successes. This is what generated complacence and was an impediment to making a principled evaluation of serious shortcomings.

Perhaps in their most glaring form negative processes stemming from an absence of criticism and self-criticism manifested themselves in Uzbekistan. Having lost touch with life the republic's former top leadership made it a rule to speak only of successes, paper over shortcomings, and respond irritably to any critical judgments. In the Republican Party organisation discipline slackened, and persons for whom the sole principle was lack of principles, their own well-being and careerist considerations were in favour. Toadyism and unbridled laudation of those 'senior in rank' became widespread. All this could not but affect the state of affairs. The situation in the economy and in the social sphere deteriorated markedly, machinations, embezzlement and bribery thrived, and socialist legality was grossly transgressed.

It required intervention by the CPSU Central Committee to normalise the situation. The republic was given all-sided assistance. Many sectors of Party, governmental and economic work were reinforced with cadres. These measures won the approval and active support of the communists and the working people of Uzbekistan.

There is something else that causes concern. The shortcomings in the republic did not appear overnight, they piled up over the years, growing from small to big. Officials from all-union bodies, including the Central Committee, went to Uzbekistan on many occasions and they must have noticed what was happening. Working people of the republic wrote indignant letters to the central bodies about the malignant practices. But these signals were not duly investigated.

The reason for this is that at some stages individual republics, territories, regions and cities were placed out of bounds to criticism. As a result, in the localities there began to appear districts, collective farms, state farms, industrial facilities and so on that enjoyed a kind of immunity. From this we have to draw the firm conclusion that in the Party there neither are nor should be organisations outside the pale of control and closed to criticism, and that there neither are nor should be leaders fenced off from Party responsibility.

This applies equally to ministries, departments and all enterprises and organisations. The CPSU Central Committee considers that the role of Party committees of ministries and departments must be enhanced significantly, that the level of their functions in restructuring the work of the management apparatus and of industries as a whole must be raised. An examination of the reports of the Party committees of some ministries in the Central Committee shows that they are still using their right of control very timidly and warily, that they are not catalysts of the new, of the struggle against departmentalism, paper-work and red tape.

The Party provides political leadership and defines the general prospect for development. It formulates the main tasks in socio-economic and intellectual life, selects and places cadres, and exercises general control. As regards the ways and means of resolving specific economic and socio-cultural problems, wide freedom of choice is given to each management body, work collective and economic cadres.

In improving the forms and methods of leadership, the Party is emphatically against confusing the functions of Party committees with those of governmental and public bodies. This is not a

General Secretary Gorbachov addressing a welcome speech to delegates and guests of the 12th World Festival of Youth and Students in Moscow on July 17, 1985.

simple question. In life it is sometimes hard to see the boundary beyond which Party control and the organisation of the fulfilment of practical tasks spills over onto petty tutelage or even substitution for governmental and economic bodies. Needless to say, each situation requires a specific approach, and here much is determined by the political culture and maturity of leaders. The Party will endeavour to so organise work that in the sector entrusted to him each person acts professionally and energetically, without fearing to shoulder responsibility. Such is the principled Leninist decision of this question and we should abide strictly by it at all levels of Party activity.

2. FOR PURITY AND INTEGRITY OF THE PARTY MEMBER, FOR A PRINCIPLED PERSONNEL POLICY

The more consistently we draw the Party's huge creative potential into the efforts to accelerate the development of Soviet society, the more tangible becomes the profound substantiation of the conclusion drawn by the April plenary meeting about the necessity of enhancing the initiatives and responsibilities of cadres and about the importance of an untiring struggle for the purity and integrity of the Party member.

The Communist Party is the political and moral vanguard. During the past five years it has admitted nearly 1,600,000 new members. Its roots in the working class, in all strata of society, are growing increasingly stronger. In terms of per hundred new members there are 59 workers and 26 trained specialists working in various branches of the economy, while of all those admitted four-fifths are young people.

By and large, the Party's composition is formed and its ranks grow in accordance with the rules, but as in any matter, the process of admittance to the Party requires further upgrading. Some organisations hasten the growth of the Party ranks to the detriment of their quality, and do not set high standards for new members. Our task is to show tireless concern for the purity of the Party ranks and dependably close the Party to uncommitted people, to those who join it out of careerist or other mercenary considerations.

We have to go on improving the ideological education of communists and insist upon stricter compliance with Party discipline and unqualified fulfilment of the requirements set by the rules. In each Party organisation the communists should themselves create an atmosphere of mutual exactingness that would rule out any possibility of anybody disregarding Party norms. In this context, we should support and disseminate the experience of many Party organisations in which communists report regularly to their comrades, and the character references given by the Party are discussed and endorsed at Party meetings. This helps to give all Party members without exception a higher sense of responsibility to their organisation.

We bear quite a lot of damage because some communists behave unworthily or perpetrate discrediting acts. Of late a number of senior officials have been discharged from their posts and expelled from the Party for various abuses. Some of them have been indicted. There have been such cases, for example, in the Alma-Ata, Chimkent and some other regions as well as in some republics, and also in ministries and departments. Phenomena of this kind are, as a rule, generated by violations of Party principles in selecting and educating cadres, and in controlling their work. The Party will resolutely go on getting rid of all who discredit the name of communist.

At our Congress I should like to say a few more words about efficiency. This is a question of principle. Any disparity between what is said and done hurts the main thing—the prestige of Party policy—and cannot be tolerated in any form. The Communist Party is a Party of unity between words and actions. This should be remembered by every leader, by every communist. It is by the unity between words and deeds that the Soviet people will judge our work.

Important resolutions have been adopted and interesting ideas and recommendations have been put forward both in the centre and in the localities since the April plenary meeting. But if we were to analyse what of this has been introduced into life and been mirrored in work, it will be found that alongside unquestionable changes much has still got stuck on the way to practical utilisation. No restructuring, no change can take place unless every communist, especially a leader, appreciates the immense significance of practical actions, which are the only vehicles that can move life forward and make labour more productive. Organisational work cannot be squandered on bombast and empty rhetoric at countless meetings and conferences.

And another thing. The Party has to declare a determined and relentless war on bureaucratic practices. Vladimir Ilyich Lenin held that it was especially important to fight them at moments of change, during a transition from one system of management to another, where there is a need for maximum efficiency, speed and energy. Bureaucracy is today a serious obstacle to the solution of our principal problem—the acceleration of the country's socio-economic development and the fundamental restructuring of the mechanism of economic management linked to that development. This is a troubling question and requires conclusions. Here it is important to bear in mind that bureaucratic distortions manifest themselves all the stronger where there is no efficiency, publicity and control from below, where people are held less accountable for what they do.

Comrades, of late many new, energetic people who think in modern terms have been appointed to high positions. The Party will continue pursuing the line of combining experienced and young cadres in the leadership. More women are being promoted to leadership positions. There are now more of them in Party and local government bodies. The criterion for all promotions and changes boils down to one thing: political qualities, efficiency, ability and actual achievements of the person concerned and the attitude to people. I feel it is necessary to emphasise this also because some people have dropped the Party traditions of maintaining constant contact with rank-and-file communists, with working people. This is what undermines the very essence of Party work.

The person needed today to head each Party organisation is one who has close ties to the masses and is ideologically committed, thinks in an innovative way, and is energetic, it is hardly necessary to remind you that with the personality of a leader, of a party leader in the first place, people link all the pros and cons of the concrete, actual life they live. The secretary of a district committee, a city committee or a regional committee of the Party is the criterion by which the rank-and-file worker forms an opinion of the Party committee and of the Party as a whole.

Cadres devoted to the Party cause and heading the efforts to implement its political line are our main and most precious asset. Party activists, all communists, should master the great traditions of Bolshevism and be brought up in the spirit of these traditions. in the Party, at each level, a principled stand and Party comradeship should become immutable norms. This is the only attitude that can ensure the Party's moral health, which is the earnest of society's health.

3. REINFORCE IDEOLOGY'S LINK TO LIFE AND ENRICH PEOPLE'S INTELLECTUAL WORLD

"You cannot be an ideological leader without...theoretical work, just as you cannot be one without directing this work to meet the needs of the cause, and without spreading the results of this theory..."*(Collected Works,* Vol. 1, p. 298.) That is what Lenin taught us.

Marxism-Leninism is the greatest revolutionary world view. It substantiated the most humane objective that humankind has ever set itself—the creation of a just social system on Earth. It indicates the way to a scientific study of society's development as an integral process that is law-governed in all its huge diversity and contraditoriness, teaches to see the character and interaction of economic and political forces, to select correct orientations, forms and methods of struggle, and to feel confident at all steep turns in history.

In all its work the CPSU proceeds from the premise that fidelity to the Marxist-Leninist doctrine lies in creatively developing it on the basis of the experience that has been accumulated. The intricate range of problems stemming from the present landmark character of the development of our society and of the world as a whole is in the focus of the Party's theoretical thinking. The many-sided tasks of acceleration and its interrelated aspects—political, economic, scientific, technological, social, cultural-intellectual and psychological—require further in-depth and all-embracing analysis. We feel a pressing need for serious philosophical generalisations founded on economic and social forecasts, on profound historical researches.

We cannot escape the fact that our philosophy and economics, as indeed our social sciences as a whole, are, I would say, in a state that is some distance away from the imperatives of life. Besides, our economic planning bodies and other departments do not display the proper interest in carrying rational recommendations of social scientists into practice.

Time sets the question of the social sciences broadly tackling the concrete requirements of practice and demands that social scientists should be sensitive to the ongoing changes in life, keep new phenomena in sight, and draw conclusions that would correctly orient practice. Viability can only be claimed by those scientific schools that come from practice and return to it enriched with meaningful generalisations and constructive recommendations. Scholasticism, doctrinairism and dogmatism have also been shackles for a genuine addition to knowledge. They lead to stagnation of thought, put a solid wall around science, keeping it away from life and inhibiting its development. Truth is acquired not by declarations and instructions, it is born in scientific discussion and debate and verified in action. The Central Committee favours this way of developing our social sciences, a way that allows reaching significant results in theory and practice.

The atmosphere of creativity, which the Party is asserting in all areas of life, is particularly productive for the social sciences. We hope that it will be used actively by our economists and philosophers, lawyers and sociologists, historians and literary critics for a bold and innovative formulation of new problems and for their creative theoretical elaboration.

But in themselves ideas, however attractive, do not give shape automatically to a coherent and active world view if they are not coupled to the socio-political experience of the masses. Socialist ideology draws its energy and effectiveness from the interaction of advanced ideas with the practice of building the new society.

The Party defines the basic directions of ideological work in the new edition of the CPSU Programme. They have been discussed at plenary meetings of the CPSU Central Committee and at the USSR practical-scientific conference held in December 1984. I shall mention only a few of them.

The most essential thing on which the entire weight of Party influence must be focused is that every person should understand the urgency and landmark character of the moment we are living in. Any of our plans would hang in the air if people are left indifferent, if we fail to awaken the labour and social vigour of the masses, their energy and initiative. The prime condition for accelerating the country's socio-economic development is to turn society towards new tasks and draw upon the creative potential of the people, of every work collective for carrying them out.

It is an indisputable fact that intelligent and truthful words exercise a tremendous influence. But their significance is multiplied a hundred-fold if they are coupled to political, economic and social steps. This is the only way to get rid of tiresome edification and to fill calls and slogans with the breath of real life.

Isolation of words from reality dramatically devalues ideological efforts. However many lectures we deliver on tact and however much we censure callousness and bureaucracy, this evaporates if a person encounters coarseness in offices, in the street, in a shop. However many talks we may have on the culture of behaviour, they will be useless if they are not reinforced by efforts to achieve a high level of culture in production, association between people and human relations. However many articles we may write about social justice, order and discipline, they will remain unproductive if they are not accompanied by vigorous actions on the part of the work collective and by consistent enforcement of the law.

People should constantly see and feel the great truth of our ideology and the principled character of our policy. Work and the distribution of blessings should be so organised and the laws and principles of socialist human association so scrupulously observed that every Soviet citizen should have firm faith in our ideals and values. Dwellings, food supplies, the quality of consumer goods and the level of health care are what most directly affect the consciousness and sentiment of people. It is exactly from these positions that we should approach the entire spectrum of problems linked to the educational work of Party and government bodies, and mass organisations.

Exceedingly favourable social conditions are created for boosting the effectiveness of ideological work in the drive to speed up socio-economic development. But nobody should count on ideological, political, labour and moral upbringing being thereby simplified. It must always be borne in mind that however conducive it may be, the present situation has its own contradictions and difficulties. No concession should be allowed in assessments.

It is always a complex process to develop the social consciousness, but the distinctive character of the present stage has made many pressing problems particularly sharp. First, the very magnitude of the task of acceleration defines the social atmosphere, its character and specific features. As yet not everybody has proved to be prepared to understand and accept what is taking place. Second, and this must be emphasised, the slackening of socio-economic development was the outcome of serious blunders not only in economic management but also in ideological work.

It cannot be said that there were few words on this matter or that they were wrong. But in practice purposeful educational work was often replaced by artificial campaigns leading propaganda away from life with an adverse effect on the social climate. The sharpness of the contradictions in life was often ignored and there was no realism in assessing the actual state of affairs in the economy, as well as in the social and other spheres. Debris of the past invariably leave an imprint. They make themselves felt, manifesting themselves in people's consciousness, actions and behaviour. Lifestyle cannot be changed in the twinkling of an eye, and it is still harder to put an end to inertia in thinking. Energetic efforts must be made there.

Policy yields the needed results when it is founded on an accurate account of the interests of classes, social groups and individuals. While this is true from the standpoint of administering society, it is even truer where ideology and education are concerned. Society consists of concrete people, who have concrete interests, their joys and sorrows, their notions about life, about its actual and sham values.

In this context I should like to say a few words about work with individuals as a major sphere of education. It cannot be said that it receives no attention, but in the ideological sphere the customary 'gross' approach is a serious hindrance. The relevant statistics are indeed impressive. Tens and hundreds of thousands of propagandists, agitators and lecturers on politics, the study circles and seminars, the newspapers and journals with circulations running into millions, and the audiences of millions at lectures. All this is commendable. But does not the living person disappear in this playing around with figures and this 'coverage'? Do not ideological statistics blind us, on the one hand, to selfless working people meriting high recognition by society and, on the other, to exponents of anti-socialist morality? That is why maximum concreteness in education is so important.

An essential feature of ideological work is also that it is conducted in a situation marked by a sharp confrontation between socialist and bourgeois ideology. Bourgeois ideology is an ideology serving capital and the profits of monopolies, adventurism and social revenge, an ideology of a society that has no future. Its guidelines are obvious: to use any device to embellish capitalism, camouflage its intrinsic anti-humaneness and injustice, to impose its standards of life and culture; by every means to throw mud at socialism and misrepresent the sense of values such as democracy, freedom, equality and social progress.

The psychological warfare unleashed by imperialism cannot be qualified otherwise than as a special form of aggression, of information imperialism impinging on the sovereignty, history and culture of peoples. Moreover, it spells out direct political and psychological preparations for war, having, of course, nothing in common with a real comparison of views or with freedom of exchanges of ideas, about which they speak hypocritically in the West. There is no other way for evaluating actions, when people are taught to look upon any society uncongenial to imperialism through a gun-sight.

Naturally, there are no grounds for overestimating the influence of bourgeois propaganda. Soviet people are quite well aware of the real value of the various forecasters and forecasts, they clearly see the actual aims of the subversive activities of the ruling monopoly forces. But we have no right to forget that psychological warfare is a struggle for people's minds, their understanding of the world, their vital, social and intellectual bearings. We are contending with a skilful class adversary, whose political experience is diverse and centuries-old in terms of time. He has built up a mammoth mass propaganda machine equipped with sophisticated technical means and having a huge apparatus of schooled haters of socialism.

The insidiousness and unscrupulousness of bourgeois propagandists must be countered with a high standard of professionalism on the part of our ideological workers, by the morality and culture of socialist society, by the openness of information, and by the incisive and creative character of our propaganda. We must be on the offensive in exposing ideological subversion and in bringing home truthful information about the actual achievements of socialism, about the socialist way of life.

We have built a world free of oppression and exploitation and a society of social unity and confidence. We, patriots of our homeland, will go on safeguarding it with all our strength, increasing its wealth, and fortifying its economic and moral might. The inner sources of Soviet patriotism are in the social system, in our humanistic ideology. True patriotism lies in an active civic stand. Socialism is a society with a high level of morality. One cannot be ideologically committed without being honest, a person with a clear conscience, decent and self-critical. Our education will be all the more productive, the more vigorously the ideals, principles and values of the new society are asserted. Struggle for the purity of life is the most effective way of promoting the effectiveness and social yield of ideological education and creating guarantees against the emergence of unhealthy phenomena.

To put it in a nutshell, comrades, whatever area of ideological work we take, life must be the starting point in everything. Stagnation is simply intolerable in a live, dynamic and many-sided matter such as information, propaganda, artistic creativity, and amateur art activity, the work of clubs, theatres, libraries and museums—in the entire sphere of ideological, political, labour, moral and atheistic upbringing.

In our day, which is replete with dynamism and changes, the role of the mass media is growing significantly. The time that has passed since the April plenary meeting of the Central Committee has been a rigorous test for the whole of the Party's work in journalism. Editorial staffs have indomitably tackled complex problems that are new in many respects. Newspapers, journals and television programmes encapsulated life with its achievements and contradictions, and there is a more analytical approach, civic motivation, and sharpness in bringing problems to light and in concrete criticism of shortcomings and omissions. Many constructive recommendations have been offered on pressing economic, social and ideological issues.

Even more significance is now being acquired by the effectiveness of the mass media. The Central Committee sees them as an instrument of creation and an articulator of the Party's general viewpoint, which is incompatible with departmentalism and parochialism. Everything dictated by principled considerations, by the interests of improving our work will continue to be supported by the Party. The work of the mass media becomes all the more productive, the more thoughtfulness and timeliness and the less pursuit after the casual and the sensational there is in it.

Our television and radio networks are developing rapidly, acquiring an up-to-date technical level. They have entered life solidly as all-embracing media carrying information and propagating and asserting our moral values and culture. Changes for the better have clearly appeared here: television and radio programmes have become more diversified and interesting, and there is a visible aspiration to surmount established stereotypes, to take the diversity of the interests of audiences into account more fully.

But can it be said that our mass media and propaganda are using all their potentials? For the time being, no. There still is much dullness, inertia has not been overcome, and deafness to the new has not been healed. People are dissatisfied with the inadequate promptness in the reporting of news, with the superficial coverage of the drive for the advanced innovations being introduced into practice. Justified censure is evoked by the low standard of some literary works, television programmes and films that suffer from a lack not only of ideological and aesthetic clarity but also of elementary taste. There has to be a radical improvement of film distribution and of book and journal publishing. The leadership of the Ministry of Culture, the State Television and Radio Committee, the State Film Committee, the State Publishing Committee of the USSR, and the news agencies have to draw effective conclusions from the innumerable critical remarks from the public. The shortcomings are common, but the responsibility is specific, and this must be constantly in the minds of ideological cadres.

The Party sees the main objective of our policy in culture in giving the widest scope for identifying people's abilities and making their lives culturally rich and many-sided. In working for radical changes for the better in this area as well, it is important to build up cultural-educational work in such a way as to fully satisfy people's cultural requirements and interests.

Society's moral health and the intellectual climate in which people live are in no small measure determined by the state of literature and art. While reflecting the birth of the new world, our literature has been active in helping to build it, moulding the citizen of that world—the patriot of the motherland and the internationalist in the true meaning of the word. It thereby correctly chose its place, its role in the efforts of the entire people. But this is also a criterion which the people and the Party use to assess the work of the writer and the artist, and which literature and Soviet art themselves use to approach their own tasks.

When the social need arises to conceptualise the time, especially a time of change, it always brings forward people for whom this becomes an inner necessity. We are living in such a time

The Reverend Jesse Jackson speaks to Mikhail Gorbachov inside the Soviet Mission in Geneva on November 19, 1985. Jackson arrived with a petition signed by Americans.

today. Neither the Party nor the people stand in need of showy verbosity on paper, petty dirty-linen-washing, time-serving and utilitarianism. What society expects from the writer is artistic innovation and the truth of life, which has always been the essence of real art.

But truth is not an abstract concept. It is concrete. It lies in the achievements of the people and in the contradictions of society's development, in heroism and the succession of day-to-day work, in triumphs and failures, in other words in life itself, in all its versatility, dramatism and grandeur. Only a literature that is ideologically motivated, artistic and committed to the people educates people to be honest, strong in spirit, and capable of shouldering the burden of their time.

Criticism and self-criticism are a natural principle of our society's life. Without them there can be no progress. It is time for literary and art criticism to shake off complacency and servility to rank, which erodes healthy morals, remembering that criticism is a social matter and not a sphere serving an author's vanity and ambitions.

Our unions of creative workers are rich in tradition, and they play a considerable role in the life of art and of the whole of society for that matter. The main result of their work is measured not by resolutions and meetings, but by talented and imaginative books, films, plays, paintings and music needed by society and which can enrich the people's intellectual life. In this context, serious consideration is merited by the suggestion from the public that the standard for judging works nominated for distinguished prizes should be raised.

Leadership of intellectual, cultural life is not a simple matter. It requires tact, an understanding of creative work, and most certainly a love of literature and art, and respect for talent. Here much depends upon the ability to propagate the Party's policy in culture, to implement it in life, on fairness in evaluations, and a well-wishing attitude to the creative work and quests of the writer, the composer and the artist.

Ideological work is creative. It has no universal means for all occasions, requires constant quest and the ability to keep abreast of life. Today it is particularly important to acquire a profound understanding of the character of present-day problems, a solid scientific world view, a principled stand, high efficiency and a sense of responsibility for work in any sector. To promote society's level of maturity and build communism means steadfastly to enhance the maturity of the individual's consciousness and enrich his intellectual world.

The Party thinks highly of the knowledge, experience and dedication of its ideological activists. Here, at our Congress, a word of the highest regard must be said to the millions of Party members who have fulfilled and continue to fulfil honourably an extremely important Party assignment in one of the main sectors of its work. We must continue to assign to ideological work comrades who by personal example have proved their commitment, are able to think analytically, and know how to hear out and talk with people, in short, highly trained in political and professional terms, and capable of successfully carrying out the new tasks of our time.

VI. THE RESULTS OF THE DISCUSSION OF THE NEW EDITION OF THE PARTY PROGRAMME AND OF THE AMENDMENTS TO THE PARTY RULES

Comrades, the political report of the CPSU Central Committee examines the Party's programme goals, its present-day economic and political strategies, the problems of improving inner-Party life and the style and methods of work, that is, all that constitutes the core of the drafts of the new edition of the Programme and of the amendments to the CPSU Rules. Therefore, there is no need to set them forth here in detail. Let me only dwell on some of the points of principle, taking into account the results of the Party-wide and nationwide discussion of the drafts of these documents.

What are these results? First of all, the conclusions and provisions of the CPSU Programme and Rules have met with widespread approval. The communists and Soviet people support the Party's policy of accelerating the country's socio-economic development and its Programme's clear orientation towards the communist perspective and the strengthening of world peace. They point out that the new historical tasks are based on in-depth analysis of the urgent problems of the development of society.

The new edition of the Programme has also evoked a wide response abroad. Progressives take note of its profoundly humane nature, its addressing itself to Man, its passionate call for mutual understanding among nations and for ensuring a peaceful future to mankind. Our friends abroad are inspired by the Soviet Union's unshakeable striving for lasting comradely relations and all-round co-operation with all the countries of the socialist world system and its firm support of the peoples' anti-imperialist struggle for peace, democracy, social progress and the consolidation of independence. Many of the sober-minded public figures in bourgeois countries take note of the peaceful orientation of our programme, of the CPSU line for disarmament and for normal, sound relations with all countries.

The preparation and discussion of the pre-Congress documents have invigorated the Party's ideological and political work and furthered the social activity of millions of working people.

The drafts of the new edition of the Programme and of the Rules have been thoroughly discussed at meetings of primary Party organisations at district, city, area, regional and territorial election conferences, and at congresses of the communist parties of union republics. Since the beginning of the discussion, over six million responses were received to the draft Programme alone. They came from workers, collective farmers, scientists, teachers, engineers, doctors, army and navy servicemen, communists and non-Party people, veterans and young people. Assessing the new edition of the Programme as a document that meets the vital interests of the Soviet people, they made numerous proposals, and suggested additions and more precise wordings. I believe it would be useful to dwell on some of them.

Stressing the novelty of the draft under discussion, the authors of some of the letters suggest adopting it at the Congress as the fourth Party Programme. It will be recalled that the adoption of new Party programmes, initially the second and then the third, was necessitated by the fact that the goals set in the preceding Programme had been reached. In our case, the situation is different.

The Party's basic tasks of developing and consolidating socialism, of its plan-governed and all-round improvement, and Soviet society's further advance to communism, remain in force. The document submitted for your consideration reiterates the theoretical and political guidelines which have stood the test of time.

At the same time, much has changed in our lives in the quarter of a century since the adoption of the Third Party Programme. New historical experience has been accumulated. Not all of the estimates and conclusions turned out to be right. Translating the tasks of the full-scale building of communism into direct practical action has proved to be premature. Certain miscalculations were made, too, in fixing deadlines for the solution of a number of concrete problems. New problems related to improving socialism and accelerating its development, as well as certain questions of international politics, have come to the fore and become acute. All this has to be reflected in the Party's programme document.

Thus, the assessment of the submitted document as a new edition of the Third Party Programme is justified in reality and is of fundamental importance. It reasserts the main goals of the CPSU, the basic laws governing communist construction, and at the same time shows that the accumulated historical experience has been interpreted in a creative manner, and that the strategy and tactics have been elaborated to suit the specificities of the present turning point.

The public have paid great attention to those provisions of the Programme which describe the stage of social development reached by the country and the goals yet to be attained through its implementation. Various opinions were expressed on this score. While some suggest that references to developed socialism should be completely removed from the Programme, others, on the contrary, believe that this should be dealt with at greater length.

The draft sets forth a well-balanced and realistic position on this issue. The main conclusions about modern socialist society confirm that our country has entered the stage of developed socialism. We also show understanding for the task of building developed socialism set down in the programme documents of fraternal parties in the socialist countries.

At the same time, it is proper to recall that the thesis of developed socialism has gained currency in our country as a reaction to the simplistic ideas about the ways and terms of carrying out the tasks of communist construction. Subsequently, however, the accents in the interpretation of developed socialism were gradually shifted. Things were not infrequently reduced to just registering successes, while many of the urgent problems related to the conversion of the economy to intensification, to raising labour productivity, improving supplies to the population, and overcoming negative things were not given due attention. Willy-nilly, this was a peculiar vindication of sluggishness in solving outstanding problems. Today, when the Party has proclaimed and is pursuing the policy of accelerating socio-economic development, this approach has become unacceptable.

The prevailing conditions compel us to focus theoretical and political thought not on recording what has been achieved, but on substantiating the ways and methods of accelerating socio-economic progress, on which depend qualitative changes in various spheres of life. An incalculably deeper approach is wanted in solving the cardinal issues of social progress. The sense of the strategy of the CPSU set out in the new edition of the Programme is centred on the need for change, for stepping up the dynamism of society's development. It is through socio-economic acceleration that our society is to attain new frontiers, whereupon the advantages of the socialist system will assert themselves to the fullest extent and the problems that we have inherited from the preceding stages will be resolved.

Divergent opinions have been expressed, too, concerning details of the programme provisions. Some people hold that the Programme should be a still more concise document, a kind of brief declaration of the Party's intentions. Others favour a more detailed description of the parameters of economic and social development. Some letters contain proposals for a more precise chronology of the periods that Soviet society will pass through in its advance to communism.

According to Lenin's principles of structuring programme documents and the ensuing traditions, the Programme should present a full-scale picture of the modern world, the main tendencies and laws governing its development, and a clear, well-argued account of the aims which the Party is setting itself and which it is summoning the masses to achieve. At the same time, however, Lenin stressed that the Programme must be strictly scientific, based on absolutely established facts, and that it should be economically precise and should not promise more than can be attained. He called for a maximum of realism in characterising the future society and the defined objectives. "We should be as cautious and accurate as possible," Lenin wrote. "...But if we advance the slightest claim to something that we cannot give, the power of our Programme will be weakened. It will be suspected that our Programme is only a fantasy." *(Collected Works,* Vol. 27, p. 148.)

It seems to me that the submitted edition of the Programme is meeting these demands. As for the chronological limits in which the programme targets are to be attained, they do not seem to be needed. The faults of the past are a lesson for us. The only thing we can say definitely today is that the fulfilment of the present Programme goes beyond the end of the present century.

The tasks that we are to carry out in the next 15 years can be defined more specifically, and have been set out in the new edition of the Programme, and in greater detail in the Guidelines for the economic and social development of the USSR until the year 2000. And, of course, the 12th five-year plan, a big step in the economy's conversion to intensive development through the acceleration of scientific and technological progress, will occupy an important place in the fulfilment of our programme aims.

Many of the responses and letters received by the Central Committee of the CPSU Commission which drew up the new edition of the CPSU Programme are devoted to social policy. Soviet people approve and support measures aimed at enhancing the people's well-being, asserting social justice everywhere, and clearing our life of everything that is contrary to the principles of socialism. They make proposals that are aimed at ensuring an increasingly full and strict fulfilment of the principle of distributing goods according to the quantity and quality of labour, and at improving the social consumption, at doing away firmly with unearned incomes and attempts at using public property for egoistic ends; at eliminating unjustified distinctions in the material remuneration of equal work in various branches of the economy, at overcoming any levelling of pay, and so on. Some of these proposals are reflected in the draft. Others must be carefully examined by Party, government and economic bodies, accounted for in legislative acts and decisions, and in our practical work.

Provisions of the Programme concerning the development of the people's socialist self-government have aroused considerable interest during the countrywide discussion. Unanimous support is expressed for the all-round democratisation of socialist society and the maximum and effective enlistment of all the working people in running the economic, social and political processes. The concrete steps taken in this field have also been commended, and ideas expressed that the capacity of work collectives as the primary cell of immediate, direct democracy should be shown more clearly when dealing with the problems of improving the administration of the affairs of society and the state. These ideas have been taken into account.

Concern for the spiritual elevation of our society prompted suggestions that the education of Soviet people should proceed more distinctly in the spirit of communist ideals and ethical norms, and struggle against their antipodes. The Programme Commission saw fit to accept these proposals, so that the principles of lofty ideological commitment and morality should imbue the content of the provisions of the Party Programme still more fully.

Something like two million people expressed their ideas concerning the CPSU Rules. Having examined the results of the discussion, the Central Committee of the Party has deemed it essential to introduce in the draft Rules a number of substantive additions and clarifications aimed at heightening the vanguard role of the Communists, the capability of primary Party organisations, at extending inner-Party democracy, and at ensuring unflagging control over the activity of every Party organisation, every Party worker.

In support of the idea of setting communists higher standards some comrades suggest carrying out a purge to free the Party of persons whose conduct and way of life contradict our norms and ideals. I do not think there is any need for a special campaign to purge the ranks of the CPSU. Our party is a healthy organism: it is perfecting the style and methods of its work, is eradicating formalism, red tape, and conventionalism, and is discarding everything stagnant and conservative that interferes with our progress; in this way it is freeing itself of persons who have compromised themselves by their poor work and unworthy behaviour. The Party organisations will continue to carry out this work consistently, systematically and unswervingly.

The new edition of the Programme and also the proposed changes in the Party Rules register and develope the Bolshevik principles of Party building, the style and methods of party work and the behavioural ethics of communists that were elaborated by Lenin and have been tried and tested in practice.

On the whole, comrades, the discussion of the CPSU Programme and Rules has been exceptionally fruitful. They have helped to amplify many ideas and propositions, to clarify formulations and to improve wordings. Allow me, on behalf of our Congress, to express profound gratitude to the Communists and all Soviet people for their business-like and committed participation in discussing the pre-Congress documents.

It is the opinion of the Central Committee of the Party that the submitted drafts, enriched by the Party's and people's experience, correspond to the spirit of the times and to the demands of the period of history through which we are now living. They confirm our Party's fidelity to the great teaching of Marxism-Leninism, they provide scientifically substantiated answers to fundamental questions of domestic and international affairs, and they give the Communists and all working people a clear perspective.

Comrades, those are the programme aims of our further development which have been submitted for the consideration of the 27th Congress.

What leads us to regard the outlined plans as being feasible? Where is the guarantee that the policy of accelerating socio-economic progress is correct and will be carried out?

The CPSU draws its strength from the enormous potentialities of socialism, from the living creating efforts of the masses. At complicated turning points in history the Leninist Party has on more than one occasion demonstrated its ability to find correct roads of progress, to inspire, rally and organise the many-million masses of working people. That was the case during the revolution, in the years of peaceful constructive endeavours, of the trials of wartime and in the difficult postwar period. We are confident this will be the case in future, too.

We count on the support of the working class because the Party's policy is their policy.

We count on the support of the peasantry because the Party's policy is their policy.

We count on the support of the people's intelligentsia because the Party's policy is their policy.

We count on the support of women, young people, veterans, all social groups and all the nations and nationalities of our Soviet motherland because the Party's policy expresses the hopes, interests and aspirations of the entire people.

We are convinced that all conscientious, honest-minded Soviet patriots support the Party's strategy of strengthening the might of our country, of making our life better, purer, fairer.

Those are the powerful social forces that stand behind the CPSU. They follow it, they have faith in the Communist Party.

The surging tide of history is now speeding towards the shallows that divide the second and third millennia. What lies ahead, beyond the shallows? Let us not prophesy. We do know, however, that the plans we are putting forward today are daring, and that our daily affairs are permeated with the spirit of socialist ethics and justice. In this troublous age the thrust of our social and, I would add, vital strategy is that people should cherish our planet, the skies above, and outer space, exploring it as the pioneers of a peaceful civilisation, ridding life of nuclear nightmares and completely emancipating all the finest qualities of Man, that unique inhabitant of the universe, for constructive efforts only.

The Soviet people can be confident that the Party is profoundly aware of its responsibility for our country's future, for a durable peace on Earth, and for the correctness of the charted policy. The main ingredients needed to put it into practice are persistent work, unity of the Party and the people, and cohesive actions by all working people.

That is the only way we will be able to carry out the great Lenin's behest to move ever forward with united vigour and resolve. History has not given us any other destiny. But what a wonderful destiny it is, comrades!

3

Speech by Mikhail Gorbachov at the Closing of the 27th CPSU Congress

It is up to history to give an objective evaluation of its importance. But already today we can say: the Congress has been held in an atmosphere of Party fidelity to principle, in a spirit of unity, exactingness, and Bolshevik truth; it has frankly pointed out shortcomings and deficiencies and made a profound analysis of the internal and external conditions in which our society develops. It has set a lofty moral and spiritual tone for the Party's activity in all spheres of life of the country.

Coming to this rostrum, delegates put all questions frankly, and did not mince words in showing what is impeding our common cause, what is holding us back. Not a few critical statements were made about the work of all links of the Party, of government and economic organizations, both at the centre and locally. In fact, not a single sphere of our life has escaped critical analysis. All this, comrades, is in the spirit of the Party's finest traditions, in the Bolshevik spirit.

More than sixty years ago, when summing up the discussion on the Political Report of the RCP(B) Central Committee to the 11th Party Congress, Lenin expressed a thought that is of fundamental importance. He said:

"All the revolutionary parties that have perished so far, perished because they became conceited, because they failed to see the source of their strength and were afraid to discuss their weaknesses. We, however, shall not perish, because we are not afraid to discuss our weaknesses and will learn to overcome them."

It is in this way, in Lenin's way, that we have acted here at our Congress. And that is the way we shall continue to act!

The Congress has answered the vital questions that life itself has put before the Party, before society, and has equipped every Communist, every Soviet citizen, with a clear understanding of the coming tasks. It has shown that we were right when we advanced the concept of socio-economic acceleration at the April 1985 Plenary Meeting.

The idea of acceleration imbued all our pre-Congress activity. It was at the centre of attention at the Congress. It was embodied in the Political Report of the Central Committee, the new edition of the Party Programme, and the amendments to the Party Rules, as well as in the Guidelines for the Economic and Social Development of the USSR for the 12th Five-Year Plan Period and for the Period Ending in the Year 2000.

These documents were wholeheartedly endorsed and approved by the delegates to the Congress.

The adopted and approved general line of the Party's domestic and foreign policy—that of the country's accelerated socio-economic development, and of consolidating world peace—is the main political achievement of the 27th CPSU Congress. From now on it will be the law of life for the Party, for its every organization, and a guide to action for Communists, for all working people.

We are aware of the great responsibility to history that the CPSU is assuming, of the huge load it has taken on by adopting the strategy of acceleration. But we are convinced of the vital necessity of this strategy. We are confident that this strategy is a realistic one. Relying on the inexhaustible potentials and advantages of socialism, on the living creativity of the people, we shall be able to carry out all the projected objectives.

To secure the country's accelerated socio-economic development means to provide new powerful stimuli to the growth of the productive forces and to scientific-technological progress through the improvement of socialism's economic system, and to set in motion the tremendous uptapped potentials of our national economy.

To secure acceleration means conducting an active and purposeful social policy by closely linking the improvement of the working people's well-being with the efficiency of labour, and by combining all-round concern for people with the consistent implementation of the principles of social justice.

To secure acceleration means to provide scope for the initiative and activity of every working person, every work collective, by deepening democracy, by steadily developing the people's socialist self-government, and by ensuring more openness in the life of the Party and society.

To secure acceleration means to bring ideological and organizational work closer to the people and direct it towards the elimination of difficulties and the practical solution of our tasks by associating this work more closely with the actual problems of life, by getting rid of hollow verbiage and didacticism, and by increasing people's responsibility for their job.

Comrades, we can and must accomplish all this!

The CPSU is entering the post-Congress period better organized, more cohesive, more efficient, with a well-considered long-term policy. It is determined to act with purpose, aware of all the complexity, the great scope and novelty of the tasks it faces, undaunted by difficulties and obstacles.

It is up to us to reach every Soviet citizen and bring home the essence and spirit of the Congress decisions. Not only must we explain its basic concepts; we must also organize in practice all work in line with present-day demands.

Very many interesting proposals were made and many profound thoughts expressed at our Congress and in the pre-Congress period. They must be carefully examined, and everything valuable and useful should be put into effect.

The most important thing now is to convert the energy of our plans into the energy of concrete action.

This was very well expressed by a delegate to our Congress, Vasily Gorin, chairman of a Belgorod collective farm.

"All over the country," he said, "in every work collective, a difficult but, we are sure, irreversible process of renovation and reconstruction is now underway. It passes through the hearts and minds of Soviet people and calls for complete dedication on the part of each and everyone. Above all in their work."

Yes, comrades, acceleration and radical changes in all spheres of our life are not just a slogan but a course that the Party will follow firmly and undeviatingly.

Many delegates noted that departmentalism, localism, paper work, and other bureaucratic practices are a big obstacle to what is new and progressive. I wish to assure you, comrades, that the Central Committee will resolutely eliminate all the obstacles standing in the way of accelerating socio-economic progress, strengthening discipline and order, and creating the organizational, moral and material prerequisites for the maximum development of creative activity, bold search, and socialist enterprise. I am confident that this will meet with broad and active support on the part of the entire Party and of all working people.

The Party committees, from top to bottom, are the organizers of the work of implementing the instructions of the Congress. What we now need is a concrete, businesslike and consistent

Soviet leader Gorbachov and French President Francois Mitterand during a ceremony upon Gorbachov's arrival in France for a four-day official visit starting October 2, 1985.

style of work, with unity of words and deeds, use of the most effective ways and means, a thorough consideration of people's opinions, and efficient coordination of the actions of all social forces.

Sluggishness, formalism, indifference, the habit of letting good ideas get bogged down in empty and endless roundabout discussions and attempts to "adjust to readjustment" must be completely overcome.

One of the main conclusions of the Congress is that all Party committees should act as genuine bodies of political leadership. In the final analysis, the success of all our efforts to implement the general line of the 27th Party Congress will be determined by the conscious participation of the broadest masses of the people in building communism. Everything depends on us, comrades! The time has come for vigorous and united actions. The Party calls on every Communist, every Soviet citizen, to join actively in the large-scale work of putting our plans into practice, of perfecting Soviet society, of renovating our socialist home.

Comrades, the congress has strongly reaffirmed that socialism and peace, and peace and constructive endeavour, are indivisible. Socialism would fail to carry out its historic mission if it did not lead the struggle to deliver mankind from the burden of military threats and violence. The main goal of Soviet policy is security and a just peace for all nations. We regard the struggle against war and military preparations, against the propagation of hatred and violence as an inseparable part of the democratization of all international relations, of the genuine normalization of all international relations, of the genuine normalization of the political climate in the world.

In one respect the nuclear danger has put all states on an equal footing: in a big war nobody will be able to stand aside or to profit from the misfortunes of others. Equal security is the imperative of the times. Ensuring this security is becoming increasingly a political issue, one that can be resolved only by political means. It is high time to replace weapons by a more stable foundation for the relations among states. We see no alternative to this, nor are we trying to find one.

Unfortunately, however, in the international community there are still some who lay claims to a special security, one that is suited only to themselves. This is illustrated by the thinking in Washington. Calls for strength are still in fashion there, and strength continues to be regarded as the most convincing argument in world politics. It looks as though some people are simply afraid of the possibility that has appeared for a serious and long-term thaw in Soviet-American relations and in international relations as a whole.

This is not the first time we have come up against this kind of situation. Now, too, the militaristic, aggressive forces would of course prefer to preserve and perpetuate the confrontation. But what should we do, comrades? Slam the door? It is possible that this is just what we are being pushed into doing. But we very clearly realize our responsibility for the destinies of our country and for the destinies of the world. We do not intend, therefore, to play into the hands of those who would like to force mankind to get used to the nuclear threat and to the arms race.

Soviet foreign policy is oriented towards a search for mutual understanding, towards dialogue, and the establishment of peaceful coexistence as the universal norm in relations among states. We have both a clear idea of how to achieve this and a concrete programme of work for maintaining and consolidating peace.

The Soviet Union is acting and will continue to act in the world arena in an open and responsible way, energetically and in good faith. We intend to work persistently and constructively to eliminate nuclear weapons, radically to limit the arms race, and to build reliable international security that is equal for all countries. A mandate to preserve peace and to curb the arms race resounded forcefully in speeches by delegates to our Congress. The Party will unswervingly carry out this mandate.

We call on the leaders of countries that have a different social system to take a responsible approach to the key issue of world politics today: the issue of war and peace.

The leadership of the CPSU and the Soviet state will do its utmost to secure for our people the opportunity to work under the conditions of freedom and a lasting peace. As reaffirmed by the Congress, our Party and the Soviet Union have many allies, supporters and partners abroad in the struggle for peace, freedom, and the progress of mankind.

We are sincerely happy to see here the leaders of the socialist countries. Allow me, on behalf of the Congress, wholeheartedly to thank the Communist Parties and peoples of these countries

Soviet leader Mikhail Gorbachov and U.S. President Ronald Regan laugh at the Geneva summit concluding ceremony on November 21, 1985.

for their solidarity with the CPSU and the Soviet Union!

For a number of the fraternal parties in socialist countries this is also a congress year. The problems and tasks that the very course of history has set before the ruling Communist Parties are similar in many respects. And by responding to them, each party contributes to the treasure-chest of world socialism's combined experience. We wish you every success, dear friends!

The CPSU is grateful for the warm greetings addressed to it by the representatives of Communist, Revolutionary-Democratic, Socialist and Social-Democratic parties, of democratic, liberation, and antiwar forces and movements. We highly appreciate their understanding and support of the idea advanced by the Congress of establishing a comprehensive system of international security and the plan for eliminating nuclear arms before the end of the century. The CPSU is convinced that they are consonant with the true interests of all nations, all countries and all humanity.

Comrades, our Congress has shown that at the present stage, which is a turning point in our country's social development, the Leninist Party is equal to its historic tasks. On behalf of the delegates representing our entire Party I should like to say from this rostrum that we Communists set great store by the confidence placed in us by the workers, the farmers, the intelligentsia, by all Soviet people. We put above all else the interests of the people, of our Motherland, of socialism and peace. We will spare neither effort nor energy to translate into life the decisions of the 27th Congress of the Communist Party of the Soviet Union.

4

Resolution of the 27th CPSU Congress

Having heard and discussed the Political Report of the Central Committee of the CPSU delivered by Comrade Mikhail Gorbachov, General Secretary of the CPSU Central Committee, the 27th Congress of the Communist Party of the Soviet Union notes that our Leninist Party has come to its Congress enriched with new experience in constructive activity, and closely united. As they carried out the programme targets of the CPSU and the decisions of the Party's 26th Congress, the Soviet people made considerable economic, social, and cultural advances. The positions of the Soviet Union in foreign affairs have grown stronger, its international prestige has risen. The CPSU is holding high the banner of struggle for peace and social progress.

At the present turning point, in a qualitatively new situation inside the country and on the world scene, the Party has again shown its loyalty to Marxism-Leninism, and its ability to deeply examine and realistically evaluate the situation, to draw the right lessons from experience, find ways of resolving the urgent problems, and overcome all that is outdated and no longer viable.

At its April 1985 Plenary Meeting, the CPSU Central Committee has thoroughly analysed the situation in the national economy and other spheres of society, and formulated the strategy of accelerating the country's socio-economic development, which won the wholehearted support of the Communists, and of all Soviet people. The Plenary Meeting courageously demonstrated the shortcomings, told the people frankly of the difficulties and deficiencies, provided powerful impulse to our advance and gave the start to a radical turn towards vigorous practical actions and a resolute tightening of discipline and heightening of efficiency.

The countrywide approval of the decisions of the Central Committee's April Plenary Meeting and of the drafts of the new edition of the CPSU Programme, the amendments to the Party Rules, and the Guidelines for the Economic and Social Development of the USSR in 1986-1990 and for the Period Ending in 2000, is evidence of a further strengthening of the unity of the Party and the people, of an extension of the Party's leading role, and offers new opportunities for fuller use of socialism's economic and spiritual potential.

The 27th Congress of the Communist Party of the Soviet Union hereby **decides:**

to approve the political course and practical activity of the CPSU Central Committee;

to approve the provisions, conclusions and tasks set forth in the Political Report of the Central Committee to the Congress, and instruct all Party organisations to take guidance in them in their work.

I

1. The Congress reaffirms and supports the analysis of the basic tendencies and contradictions in contemporary world affairs contained in the Political Report of the CC CPSU, and its evaluations and conclusions.

2. In the 20th century progress is rightly associated with socialism. World socialism is a powerful international entity. It reposes on a highly developed economy, an up-to-date scientific base, and a dependable military-political potential. Socialism is continuously demonstrating the fact

Andrei Gromyko, at left, gets a congratulatory handshake from party leader Mikhail Gorbachov after being named President on July 2, 1985. In the center is Premier Nikolai Tikhonov. In rear left are Vitaly Vorotnikov and Mikhail Solomenstev.

that social problems can be resolved on a fundamentally different, collectivist basis, and has taken the countries that follow this path to new heights of development.

Socialism is tirelessly improving social relations, augmenting its achievements purposefully, building up the power of attraction and credibility of its example, demonstrating the true humanism of our entire mode of life, and showing constant readiness to participate in broad international cooperation for peace and the prosperity of nations on an equal and reciprocal basis. By so doing, socialism is erecting an increasingly dependable barrier to the ideology and policy of war and militarism, reaction and force, to all forms of man-hating, and actively contributing to the social progress of mankind.

3. Under the impact and in the setting of the scientific and technological revolution, modern-day capitalism is making the conflict between the immensely greater productive forces and the social relations based on private ownership still more acute. We are witnessing a further exacerbation of the general crisis of capitalism. Capitalism is running into an unheard-of intertwining and mutual aggravation of all its contradictions, into a quantity of social, economic and other crises and clashes that it has never run into before in its history. It is responsible for all the main problems of our time, for the fact that they continue to exist and are becoming more acute.

In modern-day conditions one of the effects of the exacerbation of capitalism's basic contradiction, that between labour and capital, is the grave danger of a further considerable rightward shift of policy, of the entire situation in some of the leading capitalist countries.

4. In modern-day conditions, imperialism is a growing threat to the very existence of mankind. Militarism is its most monstrous offspring, seeking to subordinate the whole political machinery of bourgeois society to its influence and interests, and to exercise control of spiritual life and culture.

The responsibility for the wars and conflicts of our century, for the instigation, continuous exacerbation, and opening of new channels of the arms race, lies on imperialism and none other than imperialism. Imperialism, which was the first to use nuclear weapons, is now preparing to take a new, possibly irreparable step and carry the arms race into outer space, training the sights on the entire planet.

Imperialism has created a refined system of neocolonialism. Brutal exploitation of the developing countries is increasingly becoming an important source for financing imperialism's militarist preparations, its home policy, its very existence. Imperialism is counterposing itself more and more strongly to all mankind.

5. The course of history and of social progress requires every more insistently that states and nations constructively and positively interact on the scale of the entire planet. The combination of competition and historical contest between the two systems with the mounting tendency towards the interdependence of states within the world community is the real dialectics of modern-day world development. Through the struggle of opposites there is taking shape a controversial but interdependent, and in many ways integral, world. World affairs, their present stage, set especially rigid demands on every state—in foreign policy, in economic and social activity, and the spiritual pattern of society.

The last few decades of the 20th century confronted the nations of the world with difficult and acute problems. The need for solving the most vital global problems should prompt them to joint action, to triggering the tendency towards the self-preservation of humanity. The course of world affairs has created the requisite material, social and political conditions for this. For the Congress this is a stimulus to make decisions and actions consonant with the realities of our time.

The forces of peace and progress all over the world can neutralise the threat created by imperialism, halt the world's slide towards the edge of the nuclear abyss, and prevent outer space from becoming a battlefield. Human life, the possibilities of its all-round development, the interests of society's development rank uppermost. And to this end the Congress is directing the practical activity of the CPSU and the Soviet state.

II

1. The Party's chief sphere of activity is the economy, as it has always been. It is here that conditions are created to provide a materially and spiritually prosperous, and socially rich life for Soviet people in the setting of peace, to achieve a new qualitative state of society.

The Congress notes that in the quarter of a century since the adoption of the third Programme of the CPSU, the country's economy has moved ahead considerably. The national income has gone up nearly 300 per cent, industrial production 400, and agricultural output 70 per cent. In output of a number of key items, the Soviet Union firmly holds first place in the world. The people's well-being has improved. Real per capita incomes have gone up 160 per cent, and the social consumption funds more than 400 per cent. Most families have had their housing improved. The successes in Soviet science, education, health, and culture are universally recognised.

While giving due credit to what has been achieved, the Congress calls attention to the difficulties and the negative processes in social and economic development, which made themselves felt in the 70s and the early 80s. At that time, the rate of economic growth and of the productivity of labour had gone down visibly, some other indicators of efficiency declined, scientific and technological progress slowed down, and the imbalances in the economy became more distinct. The five-year plan targets were not being fulfilled, and social undertakings were not fully carried out. The Congress holds that the main reason for the lags was the failure to produce a timely political assessment of the change in the economic situation; the urgent and acute need for converting the economy to intensive methods of growth was not apprehended; nor was due perserverance and consistency shown in tackling the urgent matter of readjusting economic policy, the economic mechanism, the very psychology of our economic activity. Despite the effort of recent times, we have not yet managed to fully remedy the situation.

In these circumstances, the most crucial task of the whole Party and the whole country is to overcome the unfavourable tendencies in economic development firmly and to the end in the shortest possible time, to impart a high degre of dynamism to the economy, to give scope to truly revolutionary changes, and to enlist broad segments of the working people in these processes.

2. The Congress wholeheartedly approves the CPSU Central Committee's concept of accelerating the country's socio-economic development, and the practical steps towards this end. The Party's strategic course is to change to a more highly organised and more effective running of the economy with versatile and developed productive forces, mature socialist relations of production, and a smooth-working economic mechanism. The 12th five-year plan period is an important stage making for deep-going qualitative change in production.

The Congress makes it incumbent on all Party, government, economic, and mass organisations to direct all their activity to the unconditional fulfilment of the programme provision of converting the economy to the intensive way of development. The economic management at all levels must shift the emphasis from quantity indicators to quality and efficiency, from the intermediate to the end results, from expanding production capacities to their modernisation, from building up fuel and raw materials resources to improving their utilisation, and to the crash development of science-intensive industries. The structural and investment policies are to be changed accordingly.

The Party regards as the main lever for the intensification of the economy, a cardinal acceleration of science and technological progress, a broad introduction of new generations of machinery and of fundamentally new production techniques that make for the highest possible productivity and effectiveness. The foremost task set by the Congress is that of carrying out a deep-going technical reconstruction of the economy on a basis of up-to-the-minute achievements in science and technology. Each industry, enterprise and association must have a clear programme for the continuous modernisation of production. And those managers who substitute showy postures and halfhearted decisions for the real thing, and who distort the very idea of technical reconstruction, must be called strictly to account.

Engineering, which must attain the highest possible technical standards in the shortest possible time, is called upon to play the leading role in accelerating scientific and technological progress. A most important task is to develop and start up the mass production of up-to-date computers. There must be a radical reconstruction of the fuel and energy complex; the Energy Programme must be fulfilled. Much remains to be done in advancing metallurgy and the chemicalisation of the economy, in meeting the demand for new structural and other progressive materials. The Party attaches immense significance to the retooling of the industrial infrastructure, first of all

Secretary General Gorbachov makes an appearance on Soviet television to discuss arms control.

transport and communications, and also to a priority development of the light industry and other economic branches that directly meet the needs of the people.

In view of the drive aimed at reconstructing the economy, the Congress points to the need for a radical improvement of capital construction, for raising the entire building complex to a new industrial and organisational level, and substantially reducing the investment cycle.

The Congress sets the task of turning science conclusively toward the need for the economy's technical modernisation, for bringing it closer to production, using new, tested forms of integration and interaction for these purposes, speeding up the introduction of the results of research in practice, enhancing the work of Academy and sectoral institutes, of the scientific potential of higher educational establishments, and improving the training of rising generations of scientists.

3. It is the priority task of Party, government, and economic bodies, of all Communists, of all people, to perseveringly carry into effect the Party's up-to-date agrarian policy and to fulfil the Food Programme of the USSR. An effective advance is required in developing the agro-industrial complex, so as to visibly improve food supplies to the population already in the 12th five-year-plan period. It is important to secure the smooth, economically integrated functioning of all the links of the agro-industrial complex, and to enhance the impact of scientific and technological progress on the achievement of a more stable growth of agriculture and related industries.

While consistently building up the material and technical base of the agro-industrial complex, it is essential to radically improve the efficient use of the already existing powerful production potential, to concentrate efforts and resources on trends that yield the best results. Special attention should be devoted everywhere to the introduction of intensive techniques, to extending the use of collective contracts abased on genuine cost accounting, reducing losses of produce at all levels of agro-industrial production, and to building up in the shortest possible time requisite storage facilities and plant for the processing of industrial crops. The social reconstruction of the village must be speeded up, and constant conern shown for those who work in rural areas, for their working and living conditions.

These tasks will be furthered by the reorganisation and the new far-reaching measures aimed at shaping an effective managerial mechanism within the agro-industrial complex, which will provide conditions for a broad use of incentives- and profit-oriented methods in the work of its subdivisions, for a considerable extension of the independence and initiative of collective and state farms, and other enterprises, and for raising a dependable barrier to mismanagement and parasitism. Any radical change at village level calls for a serious improvement of the style and methods of management at the level of the agro-industrial complex. We must put an end to incompetent interference in the functioning of work collectives, and duplication of the work of the administrative bodies of the agro-industrial complex. In the new setting, the USSR State Agro-Industrial Committee and the Councils of Ministers of Union Republics will bear greater responsibility than before for supplying the country with food and industrial crops.

4. The policy of accelerating socio-economic development necessitates a deep-going restructuring of the economic mechanism, the shaping of an integrated, effective and flexible system of management based on the principle of democratic centralism and allowing for a fuller utilisation of socialism's possibilities. The Congress herewith instructs the Central Committee of the CPSU and the Council of Ministers of the USSR to carry through at the earliest possible time a set of measures that will put the forms and methods of economic management, abreast of current needs.

For this purpose:

—centralised guidance in securing the fulfilment of the main tasks of the Party's economic strategy must be made more efficient; at the same time we must enhance the role and independence of associations and enterprises, and also their stake in and responsibility for attaining the highest possible end results on the basis of genuine cost accounting, self-sufficiency and self-financing, and by pegging the incomes of work collectives to the efficiency of their work;

—incentives- and profit-oriented methods of management must be introduced at all levels of the economy; planning and the finance-and-credit mechanism must be improved; so must price-setting; the supply of technical equipment and materials must be restructured;

—management must get up-to-date organisational structures with an eye to the tendency towards concentration, specialisation and cooperation in production, the development of complexes of interrelated industries, territorial production complexes and other inter-industrial formations;

—an optimum combination must be secured of economic management at branch level with that at territorial level, as well as a comprehensive economic and social advancement of republics and regions, a further expansion of the rights of republican and local bodies, first of all in guiding the building industry, inter-industrial enterprises, and the social and productive infrastructures.

Any improvement of management calls for a readjustment of the mentality, a clear understanding of the new tasks by Party activists, the managerial personnel and the mass of the working people, and renunciation of prevailing stereotypes. It is essential to improve research in the theoretical aspects of management connected above all with the dialectics of the interaction of the productive forces and the relations of production under socialism, the development of socialist property, the use of commodity-money relations, and the blending of centralism with the independence of economic enterprises.

5. The Congress stresses that successful fulfilment of the projected tasks calls for the maximum mobilisation of the untapped potentialities available in the national economy. Party, government, economic and public bodies must concentrate on tightening organisation and discipline, and on combating mismanagement. The main emphasis should be laid on the full use of operating production capacities, all-out economising of raw and other materials, fuel and energy, on utilising resource-saving and wasteless production techniques, on utilising recycled materials, on making production operate more rhythmically, and on seeing to it that contract deliveries are made without fail. The maximum effort should be applied to securing a radical improvement of the quality of output and the quality of all work. Attainment of this crucial nationwide objective calls for the utmost mobilisation of the resources of all enterprises, all levels of management, with reliance on the latest achievements of science and technology. Persevering and day-to-day efforts to raise quality must become the cause of every Communist, every working person.

All economic, organisational and political work must be aimed at securing people's involvement in production as its true masters, at securing their ever more active participation in running their enterprise, enhancing the creative initiative of the working people, and organising effective socialist emulation in the drive to fulfil the 12th five-year plan targets. It is essential to enhance the role of the moral factor in stimulating frontline workers, and to step up the traditions of shock work and the Stakhanov movement.

6. The Congress attaches top importance to an active, integral social policy, to the programme of raising the standard of living, which encompasses all aspects of people's lives as projected for the 12th five-year period and the longer term. It is necessary to orientate the planning agencies and managerial bodies on the social needs, and to once and for all eliminate the underrating of the urgent problems in that sphere. Any lack of consideration for the needs of people, any impingement on their lawful interests, are impermissible on the part of officials. The Party will strictly follow the principle of social justice and will work persistently to eliminate everything that interferes with its constant implementation.

The CPSU is setting in motion a full-scale programme for raising the well-being of people to a qualitatively new level. The improvement of people's life must be indissolubly tied in with the growing labour and public activity of every working person, every production colletive.

The Congress deems it necessary to tighten control over the measure of labour and c nsumption, to peg wages and salaries more strictly to the productivity of labour, and labour's quality indicators. Levelling must be firmly eliminated, and payment of unearned money and unmerited bonuses stopped; it is essential to uncompromisingly combat unearned incomes and root out other departures from socialism's basic principle, "From each according to his ability, to each according to his work". Additional measures must be taken in the immediate future against parasites, pilferers of socialist property, and bribe-takers.

Party, government and economic bodies at the centre and locally must radically alter their attitude to the question of amply supplying the market with quality goods and services, ensuring unconditional fulfilment of the Comprehensive Programme for the Development of the Production of Consumer Goods and the Services, and increasing the contribution of every republic, territory, and region, every branch of the national economy, the work collectives, to this most important task. The responsibility of local bodies for satisfying the consumer demand must be increased.

To supply every family with a separate flat or house within the projected time, we must increase the scale of building new and modernising available housing, and encourage in every way the building of cooperatives and individual houses, and of housing for young people, and improve the housing distribution procedures.

7. Achievement of qualitative advances in the social sphere definitely presupposes deep-going changes in labour and its content, calling for a heightening of productivity, a sizable reduction of manual and unskilled jobs, and improvement of the governmental system of posting and re-posting cadres.

The Congress is setting the task of shaping a single system of uninterrupted education. For this purpose, it is essential to consistently carry out the reform of the general and vocational school, to work perserveringly in raising the effectiveness of education and upbringing, ensure that all pupils learn how to handle computers, and radically improve the training of young people for independent life and work. It is essential to restructure higher and specialised secondary education, and improve the system of training specialists and their use in production. The refresher courses and courses for the retraining of workers and specialists must be adjusted to current needs.

Cardinal measures are essential to improve health protection, mass physical culture and sports, tourism, and people's, especially young people's, rewarding leisure. The Congress notes the exceptional importance of the drive started on the initiative of the CPSU Central Committee and actively supported by the Soviet people, aimed at asserting a wholesome way of life and combatting hard drinking and alcoholism. There must be no backsliding in the struggle against this evil.

The problem of environmental protection and rational use of natural resources is acquiring great importance in the current conditions. The advantages of socialism and its plan-governed production and humane world outlook must be used to the full in resolving this global problem.

8. The Party considers it highly important to carefully examine in its policy the common basic interests of classes and social groups, and their specific interests, as an essential condition for the firm unity of Soviet society and the successful solution of the tasks of communist construction. As the Congress sees it, it is the cornerstone of CPSU policy to ensure the leading role of the working class, to strengthen the alliance of the working class, the collective-farm peasantry, and the working intelligentsia. As we improve the socialist way of life it is essential to provide the maximum opportunities for the assertion of collectivism and the development of the personality.

Measures should be carried out to further strengthen the family, heighten the responsibility of parents for the upbringing of their children, improve the working and living conditions of women so as to enable them to successfully combine motherhood with a job and public activity. It is essential to completely meet the demand of the population for children's pre-school institutions within the next few years.

It is the duty of Party and government bodies and public organisations to show daily care for war and labour veterans, and facilitate their broader participation in production and in socio-political life.

9. Faithful to the Leninist principles of its nationalities policy, the CPSU will continue tirelessly to strengthen the fraternal friendship of the peoples of our country, educate the working people in the spirit of Soviet patriotism and internationalism, and show special tact and care in everything that concerns national relations, affects the interests of each nation and nationality, and the national feelings of people; all problems arising in this sphere must be promptly resolved, and a relentless struggle conducted against any signs of nationalism, chauvinism, and localism.

It is incumbent on Party organisations to constantly care for the all-round development of the republics, to increase the contribution of each of them to the consolidation of the country's overall economic complex, to the economic power and defence capability of our multinational state, the Union of Soviet Socialist Republics.

On October 23, 1985, General Secretary Gorbachov signs the Declaration of members of the Warsaw Treaty at the final sitting of the Political Consultative Committee of the Warsaw Treaty held in Sofia, Bulgaria.

5

Mikhail Gorbachov's Message to the Conference on Disarmament

I send greetings to representatives of states who have gathered for a regular session of the Conference on Disarmament.

The Soviet Union regards its participation in the Conference on Disarmament with full responsibility as it understands that it is disarmament that constitutes the main path to asserting new and fair international structures and to building a safe world. It is disarmament that will release huge material and intellectual resources and make it possible to convert them to goals of construction, economic development and prosperity.

Mankind has reached a crucial point in its history and is faced with the choice of its further road: either overcome the inertia of the past, when security was viewed primarily through the prism of positions of strength and military-technological solutions, or remain a hostage to the race in nuclear, chemical and, in the longer term, some other no less formidable weapon.

This choice between what is prompted by reason and what leads to catastrophe can be made only by all states jointly, regardless of their social systems and economic development levels.

It must be a bold and responsible choice and its being such depends to a large extent on the states represented at the Conference on Disarmament. We can no longer limit ourselves to half-measures, which would only slow down the arms race in some areas while it would continue with a vengeance in others.

In other words, the time has come for us jointly to make big strides towards ridding the world of nuclear and other weapons so that security for everyone should mean security for all.

Taking guidance from these considerations, the Soviet Union put forward early this year a comprehensive plan, the centrepiece of which is a stage-by-stage programme of the elimination of nuclear weapons. We suggest that the sword of Damocles hanging over the peoples ever since the tragedy of Hiroshima and Nagasaki be removed once and for all before the end of this century.

It is only just that the Soviet Union and the United States, which have the largest nuclear potentials, should take the first decisive step, to be followed by the other nuclear powers.

It is our profound conviction that there is only one, direct way to rid mankind of the nuclear threat, and that is to eliminate nuclear weapons altogether. Objective realities are such that the development and deployment of 'Star Wars' weapons is bound to spur on the arms race in every area. That is why it is necessary from the outset to put an effective international ban on space strike-weapons.

Secretary General Gorbachov gives his speech at the Geneva summit closing ceremony on November 21st, 1985.

The Soviet Union suggests that chemical weapons, too, should be completely eliminated by the end of this century and that the finalisation of a convention on this problem, unduly dragged out, be given a decisive impetus.

Calling for a world without nuclear or chemical weapons, we are also prepared to go as far in reducing conventional armaments and armed forces as other states are prepared to go.

It should be stressed specifically that we suggest that all the practical measures to limit armaments and to achieve disarmament should be backed by measures of effective control and verification. The Soviet Union is as interested as any other state in being confident of strict compliance with accords.

Many provisions of our plan are directly related to the Conference on Disarmament.

Suffice it to say that the first item on its agenda is the problem of prohibiting tests, the radical solution of which, in our view, could turn the tide in the battle for the removal of the nuclear threat.

The Soviet Union for its part has been doing and continues to do everything possible to accomplish this goal. It agrees, *inter alia,* to the strictest verification of a nuclear weapon test ban, including on-site inspections and the use of every achievement of seismology.

As everyone knows, last year the USSR, wishing to set a good example, unilaterally halted all nuclear explosions, and then extended its moratorium to March 31, 1986. It now depends first and foremost on the United States whether the moratorium will continue beyond that date and whether it will become bilateral and subsequently multilateral.

It is to be hoped that the states participating in the conference raise their voices in favour of such a mode of action and that the conference itself succeeds in starting business-like talks which could lead to the complete termination of nuclear weapon tests by all, everywhere and for all time.

I wish the participants in the conference every success in accomplishing the responsible tasks facing them.

M. Gorbachov

General Secretary Mikhail Gorbachov and U.S. President Ronald Reagan at the summit meeting, which took place in Geneva from November 19th to 21st, 1985. The two leaders are shown on their way to the Soviet U.N. Mission in the Avenue de la Paix shortly before the beginning of the third round of talks.

6

Rules of the Communist Party

The Communist Party of the Soviet Union is the tried and tested militant vanguard of the Soviet people, which unites, on a voluntary basis, the more advanced, politically more conscious section of the working class, collective-farm peasantry and intelligentsia of the USSR.

Founded by V. I. Lenin as the vanguard of the working class, the Communist Party has travelled a glorious road of struggle, and brought the working class and the working peasantry to the victory of the Great October Socialist Revolution and to the establishment of the dictatorship of the proletariat in our country. Under the leadership of the Communist Party, the exploiting classes were abolished in the Soviet Union, and the socio-political and ideological unity of multinational Soviet society has taken shape and is steadily growing in strength. Socialism has triumphed completely and finally. The proletarian state has grown into a state of the entire people. The country has entered the stage of developed socialism.

The CPSU, remaining, in its class essence and ideology, a Party of the working class, has become the Party of the entire people.

The Party exists for, and serves, the people. It is the highest form of socio-political organisation, the nucleus of the political system and the leading and guiding force of Soviet society. The Party defines the general perspective in the development of the country, secures the scientific guidance of the people's creative activities, and imparts an organized, planned and purposeful character to their struggle to achieve the ultimate goal, the victory of communism.

In all its activities, the CPSU takes guidance from Marxist-Leninist teachings and its own Programme, which defines the tasks of the planned and all-round perfection of socialism and of the further progress of Soviet society towards communism on the basis of the acceleration of the country's socio-economic development.

The CPSU bases its work on unswerving adherence to the Leninist standards of Party life, the principles of democratic centralism, of collective leadership, the promotion, in every possible way, of inner-Party democracy, creative activity of the Communists, criticism and self-criticism and broad publicity.

Ideological and organisational unity, monolithic cohesion of its ranks, and a high degree of conscious discipline on the part of all Communists are an inviolable law of the CPSU. All manifestations of factionalism and group activity are incompatible with Marxist-Leninist Party principles, and with Party membership. The Party expels persons who violate the Programme and the Rules of the CPSU and compromise the lofty name of Communist by their behaviour.

The Communist Party of the Soviet Union is an integral part of the international communist movement. It firmly adheres to the tired and tested Marxist-Leninist principles of proletarian, socialist internationalism, actively promotes the strengthening of cooperation and cohesion of the fraternal socialist countries, the world system of socialism, the international communist and working class movement, and expresses solidarity with the nations waging a struggle for national and social liberation, against imperialism and for the preservation of peace.

I.
PARTY MEMBERS, THEIR DUTIES AND RIGHTS

1. Membership of the CPSU is open to any citizen of the Soviet Union who accepts the Programme and the Rules of the Party, takes an active part in communist construction, works in one of the Party organizations, carries out all Party decisions, and pays membership dues.

2. It is the duty of a Party member:

(a) to implement, firmly and undeviatingly, the Party's general line and directives, to explain to the masses the CPSU's internal and foreign policy, to organize the working people for its implementation, and to promote the strengthening and expansion of the Party's ties with the people;

(b) to set an example in labour, to protect and increase socialist property, to work persistently for raising production efficiency, for a steady growth of labour productivity, for improving the quality of output, for the application of modern achievements in science and technology and advanced know-how in the country's economic; to perfect his own qualifications, to be an active adherent to everything new and progressive, to make the utmost contribution to accelerating the country's socio-economic development;

(c) to be active in the country's political life, in the administration of state and public affairs to set an example in the fulfilment of civic duty, to promote actively the ever fuller implementation of the people's socialist self-government;

(d) to master Marxist-Leninist theory, to expand his political and cultural field of vision, and promote in all possible ways the growth of the Soviet people's consciousness and their ideological moral growth. To wage a resolute struggle against any manifestations of bourgeois ideology, private-property psychology, religious prejudices and other views and morals alien to the socialist way of life;

(e) to abide strictly by the norms of communist morality, to assert the principle of social justice which is innate in socialism, to put public interests above personal, to display modesty and decency, responsiveness and attentiveness to people, to respond promptly to working people's requirements and needs; to be truthful and honest with the Party and the people;

(f) to propagate consistently the ideas of proletarian, socialist internationalism and Soviet patriotism among the masses of the working people, to combat manifestations of nationalism and chauvinism, to promote actively the strengthening of friendship of the USSR peoples and fraternal relations with the countries of socialism, with the proletarians and working people of the whole world;

(g) to help, in every possible way, to strengthen the defence capacity of the USSR, to wage an unflagging struggle for peace and friendship among nations;

(h) to strengthen the ideological and organisational unity of the Party, to safeguard the Party against the infiltration of people unworthy of the lofty name of Communist, to display vigilance to guard Party and state secrets;

(i) to develop criticism and self-criticism, boldly lay bare shortcomings and strive for their removal, to combat ostentation, conceit, complacency and eyewash, to rebuff firmly all attempt at suppressing criticism, to resist red tape, parochialism, departmentalism and all actions injuriou to the Party and the state and to give information of them to Party bodies, up to and including the CC CPSU;

(j) to implement undeviatingly the Party's policy with regard to the proper selection of personnel according to their political and professional qualifications and moral qualities. To be uncompromising whenever the Leninist principles of the selection and education of personnel are infringed;

(k) to observe Party and state discipline, which is equally binding on all Party members. The Party has one discipline, one law, for all Communists, irrespective of their past services or the positions they occupy.

3. A Party member has the right:

(a) to elect and be elected to Party bodies;

(b) to discuss freely questions of the Party's policies and practical activities at Party meetings

›nferences and congresses, at the meetings of Party committees and in the Party press; to table .otions; openly to express and uphold his opinion as long as the Party organisation concerned as not adopted a decision;

(c) to criticize any Party organ and any Communist, irrespective of the position he holds, at arty meetings, conferences and congresses, and at the plenary meetings of Party committees. hose who commit the offence of suppressing criticism or victimizing anyone for criticism are ·sponsible to and will be penalized by the Party, to the point of expulsion from the CPSU;

(d) to attend in person all Party meetings and all bureau and committee meetings that duscuss is activities or conduct;

(e) to address any question, statement or proposal to any Party body, up to and including the 'C CPSU, and to demand an answer on the substance of his address.

4. Applicants are admitted to Party membership only individually. Membership of the Party is pen to politically conscious and active citizens from among workers, peasants, and intellectuals evoted to the communist cause. New members are admitted from among the candidate members ho have passed through the established probationary period.

Persons may join the Party on attaining the age of 18. Young people up to the age of 25 may in the Party only through the Leninist Young Communist League of the Soviet Union (YCL).

The procedure for the admission of candidate members to full Party membership is as follows:

(a) Applicants for Party membership must submit recommendations from three members of the PSU who have a Party standing of not less than five years and who know the applicants from aving worked with them, professionally and socially, for not less than one year.

Note 1. In the case of members of the YCL applying for membership of the Party, the recom- endation of a district or city committee of the YCL is equivalent to the recommendation of ne Party member.

Note 2. Members and alternate members of the CPSU Central Committee shall refrain from .ving recommendations.

(b) Applications for Party membership are discussed and a decision is taken by the general eeting of the primary Party organization; the decision of the latter is considered accepted if not ss than two-thirds of the Party members present at the meeting have voted for it, and takes fect after endorsement by the district Party committee, or by the city Party committee in cities ith no district division.

The question of admittance to the Party may be discussed without the presence of those who ave recommended an applicant for Party membership. Admittance to the Party is done, as a le, at open meetings;

(c) citizens of the USSR who formerly belonged to the Communist or Workers' Party of an- ther country, are admitted to membership of the Communist Party of the Soviet Union in con- rmity with the rules established by the CPSU Central Committee.

5. Communists recommending applicants for Party membership are responsible to Party organi- tions for the impartiality of their description of the political and professional qualifications and oral qualities of those they recommended and help them to perfect their ideological and politi- al knowledge.

6. The Party standing of those admitted to Party membership dates from the day when the eneral meeting of the primary Party organization decides to accept them as full members.

7. The procedure of registering members and candidate members of the Party, and their trans- r from one organization to another is determined by the appropriate instructions of the CC PSU.

8. If a Party member or candidate member fails to pay membership dues for three months in ccession without sufficient reason, the matter shall be discussed by the primary Party organiza- on. If it is revealed as a result that the Party member or candidate member in question has rtually lost contact with the Party organization, he shall be regarded as having ceased to be a ember of the Party; the primary Party organization shall pass a decision thereon and submit it › the district or city committee of the Party for endorsement.

9. A Party member or candidate member who fails to fulfil his duties as laid down in the Rules, r commits other offences, shall be called to account, and may be subjected to the penalty of

admonition, reprimand (severe reprimand), or reprimand (severe reprimand) with the entry in the registration card. The highest Party penalty is expulsion from the Party.

In the case of insignificant offences, measures of Party education and influence should be applied in the form of comradely criticism, Party censure, warning or reproof.

A Communist who has committed an offence must answer for it, above all, to his primary Party organization. In the event of a Communist being called to account before the Party by a superior organ, the primary Party organization will be informed about this.

When the question of calling a Party member to account before the Party is discussed the maximum attention must be shown and the grounds for the charges preferred against him must be thoroughly investigated.

The Party organization gives the Party member a hearing, no later than a year after the penalty ws imposed on him, to find out how he is rectifying his shortcomings.

10. The question of expelling a Communist from the Party is decided by the general meeting of a primary Party organization. The decision of the primary Party organization expelling a member is regarded as adopted if not less than two-thirds of the Party members attending the meeting have voted for it, and takes effect after endorsement by the district or city Party committee.

Until such time as the decision to expel him is endorsed by the district or city Party committee, the Party member or candidate member retains his membership card and is entitled to attend closed Party meetings.

An expelled Party member retains the right to appeal, within the period of two months, to the higher Party bodies, up to and including the CC CPSU.

11. The question of calling a member or alternate member of the CC of the Communist party of a Union Republic, of a territorial, regional, area, city or district Party committee, as well as a member of an auditing commission, to account before the Party is discussed by primary Party organizations; and decisions imposing penalties on them are taken in accordance with the regular procedure.

A Party organization which proposes expelling a Communist from the CPSU communicates its proposal to the Party committee of which he is a member. A decision expelling from the Party a member or alternate member of the CC of the Communist Party of a Union Republic or a territorial, regiona, area, city or district Party committee, or a member of an auditing commission, is taken at the plenary meeting of the committee concerned by a majority of two-thirds of the membership.

The decision to expel from the Party a member or alternate member of the Central Committee of the CPSU, or a member of the Central Auditing Commission of the CPSU, is made by the Party Congress, and in the interim between two congresses, by a plenary meeting of the Central Committee, by a majority of two-thirds of its members.

12. A Party member bears a double responsibility for the infringement of Soviet laws—to the state and the Party. Persons who have committed indictable offences are expelled from the CPSU.

13. Appeals against expulsion from the Party or against the imposition of a penalty, as well as the decisions of Party organizations on expulsion from the Party, shall be examined by the appropriate Party bodies within not more than two months from the date of their receipt.

II.
CANDIDATE MEMBERS

14. All persons joining the Party must pass through a probationary period as candidate members in order to more thoroughly familiarize themselves with the Programme and the Rules of the CPSU and prepare for admission to full membership of the Party. Party organizations must assist candidates to prepare for admission to full membership of the Party, and test their personal qualities in practical deeds, in fulfilment of Party and public assignments.

The period of probationary membership is one year.

15. The procedure for the admission of candidate members (individual admission, submission of recommendations, decision of the primary organization as to admission, and its endorsement) is identical with the procedure for the admission of Party members.

16. On the expiration of a candidate member's probationary period the primary Party organization discusses and passes a decision on his admission to full membership. Should a candidate member fail, in the course of his probationary period, to prove his worthiness, and should his personal traits make it evident that he cannot be admitted to membership of the CPSU, the Party organization shall pass a decision rejecting his admission to membership of the Party; after endorsement of that decision by the district or city Party committee, he shall cease to be considered a candidate member of the CPSU.

17. Candidate members of the Party participate in all the activities of their Party organizations; they shall have a consultative voice at Party meetings. They may not be elected to any leading Party body, nor may they be elected delegates to a Party conference or congress.

18. Candidate members of the CPSU pay membership dues at the same rate as full members.

III.
ORGANIZATIONAL STRUCTURE OF THE PARTY. INNER-PARTY DEMOCRACY

19. The guiding principle of the organizational structure, of the entire life and activities of the Party is democratic centralism, which signifies:

(a) election of all leading Party bodies, from the lowest to the highest;

(b) periodical reports of Party bodies to their Party organizations and to higher bodies;

(c) strict Party discipline and subordination of the minority to the majority;

(d) the decisions of higher bodies are obligatory for lower bodies;

(e) teamship in the work of all organizations and leading bodies of the Party and personal responsibility of every Communist for the fulfilment of his duties and Party assignments.

20. The Party is built on the territorial-and-production principle: primary organizations are established wherever Communists are employed, and are associated territorially in district, city and other organizations. An organization uniting the Communists of a given area is higher than any component Party organization of that area.

21. All Party organizations are autonomous in the decision of local questions, unless their decisions conflict with Party policy.

22. The highest leading body of a Party organization is the general meeting or conference (in the case of primary organizations), conference (in the case of district, city, area, regional or territorial organizations), or Congress (in the case of the Communist Parties of the Union Republics and the Communist Party of the Soviet Union). A meeting, conference or Congress are considered competent if they are attended by more than one half of the members of the Party organization or of the elected delegates.

23. The general meeting, conference or Congress elects a bureau or committee which acts as its executive body and directs all the current work of the Party organization.

An apparatus is being set up at the CC CPSU, the CCs of the Communist Parties of the Union Republics, territorial, regional, area, city and district Party committees, for doing current work on the organization and checking up on the fulfilment of Party decisions and rendering assistance to the lower organizations in their activities.

The CPSU Central Committee defines the structure and the staff of the apparatus.

24. The election of Party bodies is effected by secret ballot. Elections of the secretaries, deputy secretaries of Party organizations and Party group organizers at meetings of primary, shop or departmental organizations with less than 15 Party members and of Party groups may be held, with the consent of the Communists, by a show of hands vote. In these primary organizations the elections of delegates to district and city Party conferences are held in the same order.

In an election, all Party members have the unlimited right to challenge candidates and to criticize them. Each candidate shall be voted upon separately. A candidate is considered elected if more than one half of those attending the meeting, conference or Congress have voted for him.

The principle of systematic renewal of the composition of Party bodies and of continuity of leadership shall be observed in the election of all Party organs—from primary organizations to the CPSU Central Committee.

25. A member or alternate member of the CC CPSU, CC of the Communist Party of a Union

Mikhail Gorbachov and his wife, Raisa, with French President and Mrs. Francois Mitterand at the Elysees Palace, Paris, France.

Republic, a territorial, regional, area, city or district Party committee must by his entire activity justify the great trust placed in him by the Party. A member or alternate member of the Party committee who degrades his honour and dignity may not remain on it.

The question of the removal of a member or an alternate member of a Party committee from that body is decided by a plenary meeting of the given committee. The decision is regarded as adopted if not less than two-thirds of the members of the Party committee vote for it by secret ballot.

The question of the removal of a member of the CPSU Central Auditing Commission, or of the auditing commission of a local Party organization from this commission is decided at its meetings according to the procedure envisaged for the members and alternate members of Party committees.

26. The free and businesslike discussion of questions of Party policy in the Party, in all of its organizations is an important principle of inner-Party democracy. Only on the basis of inner-Party democracy is it possible to ensure Communists' high creative activity, open criticism and self-criticism, and strong Party discipline, which must be conscious and not mechanical.

Discussion of controversial or insufficiently clear issues may be held within the framework of individual organizations or the Party as a whole.

Party-wide discussion is held:

(a) at the initiative of the CC CPSU if it considers it necessary to consult the Party as a whole on any particular question of policy;

(b) on the proposal of several Party organizations at Republican, territorial or regional level.

Wide discussion, especially discussion on a countrywide scale, of questions of Party policy must be so held as to ensure for Party members the free expression of their views and preclude attempts to form factional groupings and to split the Party.

27. The supreme principle of Party leadership is collective leadership, which is an absolute requisite for the normal functioning of Party organizations, the proper education of cadres, and the promotion of the activity and initiative of Communists, and a reliable guarantee against the adoption of volitional, subjectivist decisions, manifestation of the cult of the individual and violations of Leninist norms of Party life.

Collective leadership presupposes personal responsibility for the assigned job and permanent control over the activity of every Party organization and every worker.

28. The CC CPSU, the Central Committees of the Communist Parties of the Union Republics, and territorial, regional, area, city and district Party committees shall systematically inform Party organizations of their work in the interim between congresses and conferences, and of the realization of the critical remarks and proposals made by Communists.

Objective and timely information of the higher Party bodies of their activities and the state of things in the localities must also be the hard and fast rule for Party committees and primary Party organizations.

29. Meetings of the active of district, city, area, regional and territorial Party organizations and of the Communist Parties of the Union Republics shall be held to discuss major decisions of the Party and to work out measures for their execution, as well as to examine questions of local significance.

30. Standing or temporary commissions and working groups on different questions of Party work may be set up at the Party committees, and other forms can also be used to draw Communists into the activities of the Party organs on a voluntary basis.

IV.
HIGHER PARTY ORGANS

31. The supreme organ of the Communist Party of the Soviet Union is the Party Congress. Congresses are convened by the Central Committee at least once in five years. The convocation of a Party Congress and its agenda shall be announced at least six weeks before the Congress.

Extraordinary Congresses are convened by the Central Committee of the Party on its own initiative or on the demand of not less than one-third of the total membership represented at the preceding Party Congress. An Extraordinary Congress shall be convened within two months and

The President and Prime Minister of France see M. Gorbachov off after his official visit in October of 1985.

is considered properly constituted if not less than one half of the total Party membership is represented at it.

The rates of representation at a Party Congress are determined by the Central Committee.

32. Should the Central Committee of the Party fail to convene an Extraordinary Congress within the period specified in Article 31, the organizations which demanded it have the right to form an Organizing Committee which shall enjoy the powers of the Central Committee of the Party in respect of the convocation of the Extraordinary Congress.

33. The Congress:

(a) hears and approves the reports of the Central Committee, of the Central Auditing Commission, and of the other central organizations;

(b) reviews, amends and endorses the Programme and the Rules of the Party;

(c) determines the line of the Party in matters of home and foreign policy, and examines and decides the most important questions of Party and state life, of communist construction;

(d) elects the Central Committee and the Central Auditing Commission.

34. The number of members to be elected to the Central Committee and to the Central Auditing Commission is determined by the Congress. In the event of vacancies occurring in the Central Committee, they are filled from among the alternate members of the CC CPSU.

35. In the interim between congresses, the Central Committee of the Communist Party of the Soviet Union directs the activities of the Party, the local Party bodies, selects and appoints leading functionaries, directs the work of central government bodies and public organizations of working people, sets up various Party organs, institutions and enterprises, and directs their activities, appoints the editors of the central newspapers and journals operating under its control, and distributes the funds of the Party budget and controls its execution.

The Central Committee represents the CPSU in its relations with other Parties.

36. The Central Auditing Commission of the CPSU supervises the observance of the established procedure of handling of affairs, the work done on considering the letters, applications and complaints from the working people in the Party's central organs, and audits the correctness of execution of the Party budget, including the payment, collection and accounting of Party dues, and also the financial and economic activities of the enterprises and offices of the CPSU Central Committee.

37. The CC CPSU shall hold not less than one plenary meeting every six months. Alternate members of the Central Committee shall attend its plenary meetings with consultative voice.

38. The Central Committee of the Communist Party of the Soviet Union elects a Politbureau to direct the work of the Party between plenary meetings of the and a Secretariat to direct current work, chiefly the selection of cadres and the verification of the fulfilment of Party decisions. The Central Committee elects the General Secretary of the CC CPSU.

39. The Central Committee of the Communist Party of the Soviet Union organizes the Party Control Committee of the CC.

The Party Control Committee of the CC CPSU:

(a) verifies the observance of Party discipline by members and candidate members of the CPSU, and takes action against Communists who violate the Programme and the Rules of the Party, and Party or state discipline, and against violators of Party ethics;

(b) considers appeals against decisions of Central Committees of the Communist Parties of the Union Republics or of territorial and regional Party committees to expel members from the Party or impose penalties upon them.

40. Between Party congresses the CPSU Central Committee can convene, if the need arises, an All-Union Party Conference to discuss topical questions concerning Party policy. The order of holding an All-Union Party Conference is determined by the CC CPSU.

V. REPUBLICAN, TERRITORIAL, REGIONAL, AREA, CITY AND DISTRICT ORGANIZATIONS OF THE PARTY

41. The Republican, territorial, regional, area, city and district Party organizations and their committees take guidance in their activities from the Programme and the Rules of the CPSU,

conduct all work for the implementation of Party policy and organize the fulfilment of the directives of the CC CPSU within the Republics, territories, regions, areas, cities and districts concerned.

42. The basic duties of Republican, territorial, regiona, area, city and district Party organizations, and of their leading bodies are:

(a) political and organizational work among the masses, mobilization of the Communists and all working people for the fulfilment of the tasks of communist construction, the acceleration of socio-economic development on the basis of scientific and technological progress, for raising the effectiveness of social production and labour productivity, improving the quality of output, for the fulfilment of state plans and socialist obligations, ensurance of the steady improvement of the material and cultural standards of the working people;

(b) organization of ideological work, propaganda of Marxism-Leninism, promotion of the communist awareness of the working people, guidance of the local press, radio and television, and control over the activities of scientific, cultural and educational institutions;

(c) guidance of Soviets of People's Deputies, trade union, YCL, cooperative and other public organizations through the Communists working in them, and increasingly broader enlistment of working people in the activities of these organizations, development of the initiative and activity of the masses as an essential condition for the further in-depth development of socialist democracy.

(d) strict observance of the Leninist principles and methods of management, the consolidation of the Leninist style in Party work, in all spheres of state and economic management, securing the unity of ideological, organizational and economic activities, the strengthening of socialist legality, state and labour discipline, order and organization in all sectors;

(e) conducting the cadres policy, education of the personnel in the spirit of communist ideology, moral purity, a high sense of responsibility to the Party and the people for the work entrusted to them;

(f) organization of various institutions and enterprises of the Party within the bounds of their Republic, territory, region, area, city or district, and guidance of their activities; distribution of Party funds within the given organization; systematic information of the higher Party body and accountability to it for their work.

Leading bodies of Republican, territorial and regional Party organizations

43. The highest body of Republican, territorial and regional Party organizations is the Congress of the Communist Party of the Union Republic and the respective territorial or regional Party conference, and in the interim between them, the Central Committee of the Communist Party of the Union Republic and the territorial or regional committee.

44. A regular Congress of the Communist Party of the Union Republic is convened by the Central Committee of the Communist Party at least once in five years. Regular territorial and regional Party conferences are convened by the respective territorial or regional committees once every two-three years. Extraordinary congresses and conferences are convened by decision of the Central Committee of the Communist Party of the Union Republic, or territorial or regional committees, or on the demand of one-third of the total membership of the organizations belonging to the Republican, territorial or regional Party organization.

The rates of representation at congresses of the Communist Parties of the Union Republics and at territorial and regional conferences are determined by the respective Party committees.

Congresses of the Communist Parties of the Union Republics, and territorial and regional conferences, hear the reports of the Central Committee of the Communist Party of the Union Republic, or the respective territorial or regional committees, and of the auditing commission, discuss at their own discretion other matters of Party, economic and cultural development, and elect the Central Committee of the Communist Party of the Union Republic, the territorial or regional committee, the auditing commission and the delegates to the Congress of the CPSU.

Between congresses of the Communist Parties of the Union Republics the Central Committees of the Communist Parties can convene, if the need arises, Republican Party conferences to discuss topical questions concerning Party organizations' activities. The order of holding them is determined by the Central Committees of the Communist Parties of the Union Republics.

45. The Central Committees of the Communist Parties of the Union Republics and the territorial and regional committees elect bureaus, which also include secretaries of the committees. The secretaries must have a Party standing o fnot less than five years. The plenary meetings of the committees confirm the heads of departments of these committees, the chairmen of Party control commissions, editors of Party newspapers and journals.

The Central Committees of the Communist Parties of the Union Republics, territorial and regional Party committees set up secretariats to examine current business and verify the execution of decisions.

46. The plenary meetings of the Central Committees of the Communist Parties of the Union Republics and territorial and regional committees shall be convened at least once every four months.

47. The Central Committee of the Communist Parties of the Union Republics and the territorial and regional committees direct the area, city and district Party organizations, inspect their work and regularly hear reports of the respective Party committees.

Party organizations in Autonomous Republics, and in autonomous and other regions forming part of a Union Republic or a territory function under the guidance of the Central Committees of the Communist Parties of the Union Republics or the respective territorial committees.

Leading bodies of area, city and district (urban and rural) Party organizations

48. The highest body of an area, city or district Party organization is the area, city and district Party conference or the general meeting of Communists convened by the area, city or district committee once in two-three years, and the extraordinary conference convened by decision of the respective committee or on the demand of one-third of the total membership of the Party organization concerned.

Gorbachov arrived in Paris on October 2, 1985 on an official visit at the invitation of French President Mitterand.

Gorbachov and Mitterand during their joint press conference.

The area, city or district conference (general meeting) hears reports of the committee and auditing commission, discusses at its own discretion other questions of Party, economic and cultural development, and elects the area, city and district committee, the auditing commission and delegates to the regional and territorial conference or the Congress of the Communist Party of the Union Republic.

The rates of representation to the area, city or district conference are determined by the respective Party committee.

49. The area, city or district committee elects a bureau, including the committee secretaries, and confirms the appointment of heads of committee departments, chairman of the Party commission and newspaper editors. The secretaries of the area, city and district committees must have a Party standing of at least five years. The committee secretaries are confirmed by the respective regional or territorial committee, or the Central Committee of the Communist Party of the Union Republic.

50. The area, city and district committee organizes the primary Party organizations, direct their work, regularly hears reports concerning the work of Party organizations, and keeps a register of Communists.

51. The plenary meeting of the area, city and district committee is convened at least once in three months.

VI.
PRIMARY PARTY ORGANIZATIONS

52. Primary Party organizations are the basis of the Party.

Primary Party organizations are formed at the places of work of Party members—in factories, state farms and other enterprises, collective farms, units of the Armed Forces, offices, educational establishments, etc., wherever there are not less than three Party members. Should the necessity arise, primary Party organizations may also be organized on the residential principle.

In individual cases, with the sanction of the regional, territorial committee, or the Central Committee of the Communist Party of the Union Republic, Party organizations may be formed within the framework of several enterprises that form a production association and are located, as a rule, on the territory of one or several districts in the same city.

53. At enterprises, collective farms and institutions with over 50 Party members and candidate members of the CPSU, shop, sectional, farm, team, departmental, etc., Party organizations may be formed as units of the general primary Party organization with the sanction of the district, city or area committee.

Within shop, sectional, etc., organizations and also within primary Party organizations having less than 50 members and candidate members, Party groups may be formed in the teams and other production units.

54. The highest organ of the primary Party organization is the Party meeting, which is convened at least once a month. In Party organizations with shop or departmental Party organizations, both general and shop or departmental meetings are convened at least once in two months.

In large Party organizations with a membership of more than 300 Communists, a general Party meeting is convened when necessary at times fixed by the Party committee or on the demand of a number of shop or departmental Party organizations.

55. For the conduct of current business the primary, shop or departmental Party organization elects a bureau for the term of two or three years. The number of its members is fixed by the Party meetings. Primary, shop and departmental Party organizations with less than 15 Party members do not elect a bureau. Instead, they elect a secretary and deputy secretary of the Party organization. Elections in these organizations are held every year.

Secretaries of primary, shop and departmental Party organizations must have a Party standing of at least one year.

Primary Party organizations with less than 150 Party members shall have, as a rule, no salaried functionaries released from their regular work.

56. In large factories and offices with more than 300 members and candidate members of the Party, and in exceptional cases in factories and offices with over 100 Communists, by virtue of special production conditions and territorial disconnection, subject to the approval of the regional committee, territorial committee or Central Committee of the Communist Party of the Union Republic, Party committees may be formed, the shop and departmental organizations being granted the status of primary Party organizations.

In Party organizations of collective farms, state farms and other agricultural enterprises Party committees may be formed if they have 50 Communists.

In Party organizations with over 500 Communists Party committees may be formed in large shops in individual cases with the sanction of the regional committee, territorial committee or Central Committee of the Communist Party of the Union Republic, and the Party organizations of production sections may be granted the status of primary Party organizations.

The Party committees are elected for the term of 2-3 years. Their numerical composition is fixed by the general Party meeting or conference.

Party committees, Party bureaus, secretaries of primary, shop or departmental Party organizations systematically inform Communists of their work at Party meetings.

57. Party Central Committees of primary Party organizations with more than 1,000 Communists may be granted, with the sanction of the Central Committee of the Communist Party of the Union Republic, the powers of a district Party committee in matters of admission of new members to the CPSU, keeping a register of members and candidate members of the Party and consideration of personal cases of Communists.

These organizations may elect enlarged Party committees within which bureaus are formed to guide day-to-day work.

58. In its activities the primary Party organization takes guidance from the Programme and the Rules of the CPSU. It is the political nucleus of a work collective, it conducts its work directly among the working people, rallies them round the Party, organizes them to fulfil tasks of communist construction, takes an active part in implementing the Party's cadres policy.

The primary Party organization:

(a) admits new members to the CPSU;

(b) educates Communists in a spirit of loyalty to the Party cause, ideological staunchness and communist ethics;

(c) organizes the study by Communists of Marxist-Leninist theory in close connection with the practice of communist construction and combats any manifestations of bourgeois ideology, revisionism and dogmatism, backward views and moods;

(d) takes care of raising the vanguard role of Communists in the sphere of labour and socio-political activities, and their exemplary behaviour in everyday life, and hears reports from members and candidate members of the CPSU about their fulfilment of the duties required by the Rules and Party assignments;

(e) acts as the organizer of the working people for the solving of tasks of economic and social development, heads the socialist emulation movement for the fulfilment of state plans and undertakings, the intensification of production, the raising of labour productivity and quality of products, the introduction on a broad scale into production of achievements of science and technology, of advanced experience, rallies the working people to disclose untapped resources, works to achieve the rational, economical use of material, labour and financial resources, shows concern for the protection and increase of public wealth, for improving conditions of people's work and daily life;

(f) conducts agitational and propaganda work, educates the working people in the spirit of devotion to the ideas of communism, Soviet patriotism and peoples' friendship, helps them to cultivate high-standard political culture and enhances their social activity and responsibility.

(g) works to foster in Communists and all working people the habits of taking part in socialist self-government, ensures the enhancement of the role of the work collective in running the affairs of enterprises and institutions, directs the work of trade union, YCL and other public organizations.

(h) on the basis of extensive spread of criticism and self-criticism, combats cases of bureaucracy, parochialism, departmentalism, violations of state, labour and production discipline, thwarts attempts to deceive the state, acts against negligence, waste and extravagance, strives to vindicate a sobriety.

59. Primary Party organizations of enterprises of industry, transport, communication, construction, material and technical supplies, trade, public catering, communal and other services, collective and state farms and other agricultural enterprises, design organizations, drafting offices, research institutes, educational establishments, cultural and medical institutions, enjoy the right to control the work of the administration.

The Party organizations at ministries, state committees, and other central or local government, economic agencies and departments exercise control of how the apparatus fulfils the directives of the Party and government and observes Soviet laws. They must actively promote improvement of the apparatus, the selection, placing and education of its personnel, enhance their sense of responsibility for work entrusted to them, for the development of the branch, the servicing of the population, promote state discipline, firmly combat bureaucracy and red tape, inform the appropriate Party bodies in good time on shortcomings in the work of the respective offices and individuals, regardless of what posts the latter may occupy.

Note. Primary Party organizations may set up commissions to exercise the right to control the administration's activities, and the work of the apparatus in separate avenues of production activity.

VII.
THE PARTY AND THE STATE AND PUBLIC ORGANIZATIONS

60. The CPSU, acting in the framework of the Constitution of the USSR, exercises political guidance over the state and public organizations, directs and coordinates their work.

The Party organizations and the Communists who work in state and public organizations ensure that these organizations should in full measure exercise their powers under the Constitution, the rights and duties under the Rules, and draw the working people on a wide scale into management and the solution of political, economic and social questions.

Party organizations are not a substitute for the government, trade union, cooperative and other public organizations, and do not allow the mixing of the functions of the Party and other organs.

61. Party groups are formed at congresses, conferences, meetings convened by state and public organizations, as well as at the elected organs of these organizations, having at least three Party members. The task of these groups is to carry out the Party's policy in the corresponding non-Party organizations, increase the influence of Communists on the state of affairs in these organizations, promote the democratic norms of their activities, strengthen Party and state discipline, combat red tape, and check up on the fulfilment of Party and government directives.

62. The work of the Party groups within non-Party organizations is directed by a corresponding Party organ: the CPSU Central Committee, the Central Committee of the Communist Party of the Union Republic, territorial, regional, area, city, district Party committee.

VIII.
THE PARTY AND THE YCL

63. The Leninist Young Communist League of the Soviet Union is an independently acting social and political organization of young people, an active helper and reserve of the Party. The YCL helps the party to educate the youth in the communist spirit, draw it into the work of building a new society, into the management of state and public affairs, to mould a generation of harmoniously developed people who are ready for labour and defence of the Soviet Motherland.

64. The YCL organizations must be active levers in the implementation of Party directives in all spheres of production and public life. They enjoy the right of broad initiative in discussing and submitting to the appropriate Party organizations questions related to the work of enterprises, collective farms, offices and educational establishments, take a direct part in solving them, especially if they pertain to work, everyday life, teaching and educating of young people.

65. The YCL conducts its activities under the guidance of the Communist Party of the Soviet Union. The work of the local YCL organizations is directed and controlled by the appropriate Republican, territorial, regional, area, city and district Party organizations.

In their communist educational work among the youth, in rallying it for the fulfilment of specific tasks of production and social life, local Party bodies and primary Party organizations rely on the support of the YCL organizations, uphold their useful initiatives, give every assistance in their activity.

66. Members of the YCL who have been admitted into the CPSU cease to belong to the YCL the moment they join the Party, provided they are not members of elected YCL organs and do not work as YCL functionaries.

IX.
PARTY ORGANIZATIONS IN THE ARMED FORCES

67. Party organizations in the Armed Forces take guidance in their work from the Programme and the Rules of the CPSU and operate on the basis of instructions approved by the Central Committee. They carry out the policy of the Party in the Armed Forces, rally servicement round the Communist Party, educate them in the spirit of Marxism-Leninism and boundless loyalty to the socialist homeland, actively further the unity of the army and the people, take care to raise the combat preparedness of troops, work for the strengthening of military discipline, rally servicemen to carry out the tasks of combat training and political education and acquire skill in the use of new materiel and weapons, and to irreproachably perform their military duty and the orders and instructions of the command.

68. The guidance of Party work in the Armed Forces is exercised by the Central Committee of the CPSU through political bodies. The Chief Political Administration of the Soviet Army and Navy functions as a department of the CC CPSU.

During May of 1985 Gorbachov laid a wreath at the monument to inhabitants and soldiers who died in Leningrad during World War II.

ЛЕНИНГРАДЦЫ
СОЛДАТЫ-КРАСНОАРМЕЙЦЫ
ЖИЗНЬЮ СВОЕЮ
ТЕБЯ, ЛЕНИНГРАД
РЕВОЛЮЦИИ.
МЫ ЗДЕСЬ ПЕРЕЧИСЛИТЬ НЕ СМОЖЕМ
ОХРАНОЙ ГРАНИТА
ЭТИМ КАМНЯ
И НИЧТО НЕ ЗАБЫ
РАБОЧИЕ
ОДНОЙ ВАШЕЙ ЖИЗНИ ТОВАРИЩИ
ПОДВИГ СВОЙ
ВЫ СВЕРШАЛИ
ВЫ ВСЕ ОДЕРЖАЛИ
ТАК ПУСТЬ ЖЕ ПРЕД ЖИЗНЬЮ
СКЛОНЯЕТ ЗНАМЕНА НАРОД
МАТЬ И ГОРОД-ГЕРОЙ

The chiefs of the political administrations of military districts and fleets, and chiefs of the political department of armies, flotillas and formations must be Party members of five years' standing.

69. The Party organizations and political bodies of the Armed Forces maintain close contact with local Party committees, and keep them informed about political work in the military units. The secretaries of military Party organizations and chiefs of political bodies participate in the work of local Party committees.

X.
PARTY FUNDS

70. The funds of the Party and its organizations are derived from membership dues, incomes from Party enterprises and other revenue.

The manner in which Party funds are to be used is decided upon by the CPSU Central Committee.

71. The monthly membership dues for Party members and candidate members are as follows:

Monthly earnings	Dues	
up to 70 roubles	10 kopeks	
from 71 to 100 roubles	20 kopeks	
from 101 to 150 roubles	1.0 per cent	of the monthly earnings
from 151 to 200 roubles	1.5 per cent	of the monthly earnings
from 201 to 250 roubles	2.0 per cent	of the monthly earnings
from 251 to 300 roubles	2.5 per cent	of the monthly earnings
over 300 roubles	3.0 per cent	of the monthly earnings

72. An entrance fee of 2 per cent of the monthly earnings is paid on admission to the Party as a candidate member.

Soviet leader Mikhail Gorbachov relating his position on one of the topics of discussion at the Geneva summit in November, 1985.

President Reagan and General Secretary Gorbachov greet each other in Geneva, Switzerland.

7

Geneva—The United States-Soviet Summit, November 1985

Background

Any meeting between an American President and his Soviet counterpart is an impressive historical event, often compared to a medieval jousting match or the combat of Roman gladiators. The first Reagan-Gorbachov summit, which took place in Geneva on November 19-21, 1985, was perhaps even more dramatic and eagerly awaited than previous encounters between superpower chiefs. The reasons for this are clear: Not since Jimmy Carter met with Leonid Brezhnev in Vienna in 1979 had White House and Kremlin leaders sat down to talk. The summit, if it would not immediately resolve the most pressing East-West conflicts, would at least be an improvement over six years of chilled silence and would be the first step towards establishing an ongoing dialogue that could ultimately lead to a breakthrough in U.S.-Soviet relations. In addition, the charismatic personalities and obvious strength of both leaders heightened the world's perception of the meeting as a contest between two very formidable champions.

The Geneva meeting was preceded by a series of preparatory summit briefings, conferences, speeches, and publicity in both Washington and Moscow. During the week before the summit, U.S. Secretary of State George Schultz, National Security Advisor Robert McFarlane, and Ambassador to Moscow Arthur Hartman met in Osobynak with Soviet Foreign Minister Eduard Shevardnadze and Soviet Ambassador to Washington Anatoly Dobrynin in order to plan the agenda for the Geneva meeting. The most important of the designated 26 issues were in the areas of Security Issues (Strategic Weapons, Intermediate Range Nuclear Forces, Space Weapons, Nuclear Nonproliferation), Regional Conflicts, Bilateral Issues, and Human Rights.

Those who attended the Geneva meeting included, on the American side, George Schultz, Robert McFarlane, Arthur Hartman, White House Chief of Staff Donald Regan, Special Advisor to the President for arms Control Paul Nitze, Assistant Secretary of State for European Affairs Rosanne Ridgeway, and Special Assistant to the President for National Security Affairs Jack Matlock. On the Soviet side, attending the meeting were Eduard Shevardnadze, Anatoly Dobrynin, First Deputy Foreign Minister Georgy Kornienko, Head of the Propaganda Department of the CPSU Central Committee Alexander Yakovlev, Head of the National Information Department of the CSPU Central Committee Leonid Zamyatin, *and* Assistant to the General Secretary of the CPSU Central Committee Andrei Alexandrov.

Mikhail GORBACHOV's Speech at the Closing Ceremony

The President and I have done a great deal of work. We discussed in a thorough, profound way and with straightforwardness and frankness a number of major problems concerning relations between our countries and the present-day situation in the world. These are problems whose solution concerns most closely the interests of our peoples, as well as the peoples of many other countries.

We discussed them proceeding from the intention, confirmed by both sides, to improve relations between the USSR and the USA, to help reduce the threat of nuclear war, to prevent a race in space-strike arms and to stop the arms race on earth.

We regard such discussion as useful in itself. Its results are reflected quite fully in the Joint Statement agreed on by the sides.

We must be realists and say frankly: it has not proved possible at this meeting to find solutions to the most important issues connected with the task of halting the arms race and strengthening peace, and there remain major disagreements on fundamental issues between us. But the President and I have agreed that the effort to find mutually acceptable solutions to these most important issues will be continued with perseverance here in Geneva by our representatives.

A search will also be carried out for new forms of developing bilateral Soviet-US relations. There will also be further consultations on a number of regional problems on which our positions in most cases are totally different.

We regard agreement on all these future discussions as useful.

But the real importance of everything which the President and I have agreed on can manifest itself only in concrete, practical deeds. If we really want to achieve something, it is necessary that both sides should do a great deal of work in the spirit of the Joint Statement we have adopted.

I want to say in this connection that the Soviet Union, for its part, will make every effort, in cooperation with the United States of America, to find a practical solution to the problems of curbing the arms race, reducing the stockpiled arsenals and ensuring conditions for a lasting peace between our peoples, a durable peace on earth and in outer space.

We say this, being fully aware of our responsibility to our own people and to the other peoples of the world, and would like very much to be able to count on a similarly responsible approach on the part of the US Administration. In that case the work done in Geneva these days will not be in vain.

In conclusion I would like to thank wholeheartedly the Government of Switzerland for the conditions it created for our work.

Ronald REAGAN's Speech at the Closing Ceremony

May I express Nancy's and my deep personal appreciation and that of all Americans to the people of Switzerland for welcoming us so warmly and preparing the foundations for productive discussions. Yours is a long and honorable tradition of promoting international peace and understanding. You should take pride in being the capital for international discussions. So, again, to the government of Switzerland and to the citizens of Geneva, many, many thanks.

We've packed a lot into the last two days. I came to Geneva to seek a fresh start in relations between the United States and the Soviet Union and we have done this. General Secretary Gorbachev and I have held comprehensive discussions covering all elements of our relationship. I'm convinced that we are heading in the right direction. We've reached some useful interim results which are described in the Joint Statement that is being issued this morning.

In agreeing to accelerate the work of our nuclear arms negotiators, Mr. Gorbachev and I have addressed our common responsibility to strengthen peace. I believe that we have established a process for more intensive contacts between the United States and the Soviet Union. These two days of talks should inject a certain momentum into our work on the issues between us—a momentum we can continue at the meeting that we have agreed on for next year.

Before coming to Geneva, I spoke often of the need to build confidence in our dealings with each other. Frank and forthright conversation at the summit are part of this process. But I'm certain General Secretary Gorbachev would agree that real confidence in each other must be built on deeds, not simply words. This is the thought that ties together all the proposals that the

United States has put on the table in the past and this is the criteria by which our meetings will be judged in the future.

The real report card on Geneva will not come in for months or even years. But we know the questions that must be answered. Will we join together in sharply reducing offensive nuclear arms and moving to non-nuclear defensive strengths, for systems to make this a safer world? Will we join together to help bring about a peaceful resolution of conflicts in Asia, Africa, and Central America so that the peoples there can freely determine their own destiny without outside interference? Will the cause of liberty be advanced and will the treaties and agreements signed—past and future—be fulfilled? The people of America, the Soviet Union, and throughout the world are ready to answer yes.

I leave Geneva today and our fireside summit determined to pursue every opportunity to build a safer world of peace and freedom. There's hard work ahead, but we're ready for it. General Secretary Gorbachev, we ask you to join us in getting the job done, as I'm sure you will.

Outcome

At the summit, the leaders of the United States and the Soviet Union recognized that any conflict between their two countries would have catastophic results, and they emphasized the importance of preventing any war between them, whether nuclear or conventional. They agreed to accelerate negotiations on nuclear and space-based weapons. Both leaders reaffirmed their commitment assumed by them under the Treaty of the Non-proliferation of Nuclear Weapons, to pursue negotiations in accordance with Article VI of the Treaty. They agreed to increase efforts to conclude an effective and verifiable international convention on the prohibition of nuclear weapons and the destruction of the existing stockpiles of such weapons. Both the U.S. and the Soviet Union expressed willingness to work for positive results in the area of reduction of armed forces and armaments in Central Europe.

President Reagan and General Secretary Gorbachov resolved to expand programs of bilateral cultural, educational and scientific–technical exchanges, and also to deveplop trade and economic ties. They agreed to contribute to the preservation of the environment through joint research and practical measures.

Naturally, serious differences remain on the number of highly critical U.S.–Soviet issues. However, both sides confirmed the importance of an ongoing dialogue, and at the time of this printing arrangements are being made for a second summit in late 1986, to be held in the United States.

The Gorbachovs and the Reagans, with translators, in conversation.

Mikhail Gorbachov discusses the Chernobyl accident on Soviet television.

TV Address By Mikhail Gorbachov On The Chernobyl Disaster

May 15, 1986

Good evening, comrades,

As you all know, misfortune has befallen us—the accident at the Chernobyl nuclear power plant. It has brought pain to Soviet people and stirred the international community. For the first time ever we encountered in reality such a formidable force as nuclear energy that has gone out of control. On considering the extraordinary and dangerous nature of what happened in Chernobyl, the Politbureau took into its hands the organization of work to ensure the speediest correction of the breakdown and the limitation of its consequences. A Government commission was formed which immediately left for the scene of the accident while at the Politbureau a group was formed under Nikolai Ivanovich Ryzhkov to solve problems of great urgency.

Work is being conducted around the clock. The scientific, technical and economic possibilities of the entire country have been put to use. Operating in the area of the accident are organizations of many Union Ministries and departments led by Ministers, prominent scientists and specialists, units of the Soviet Army and the Ministry of Internal Affairs.

cordial leave-taking between President Reagan and Party General Secre-

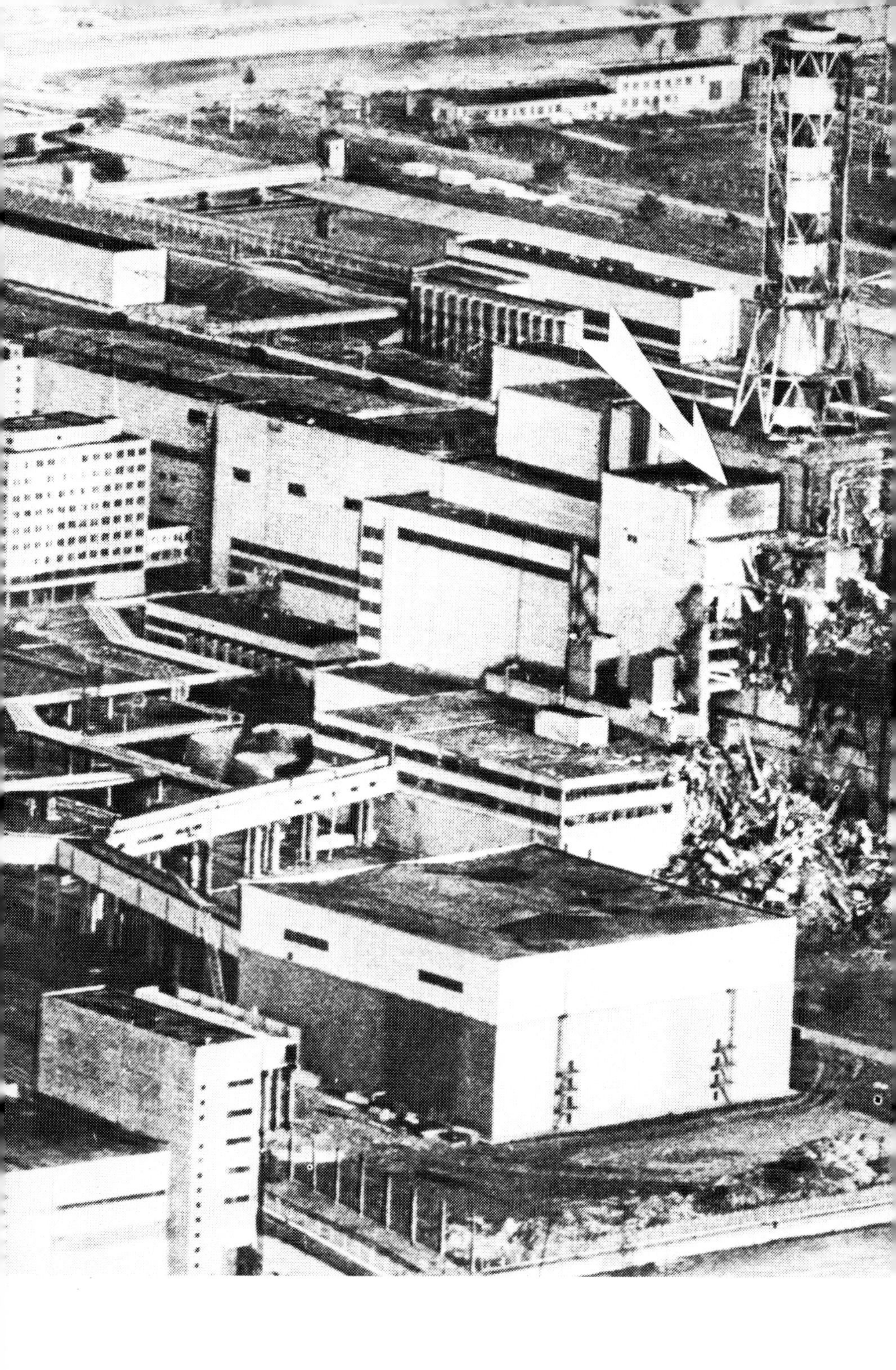

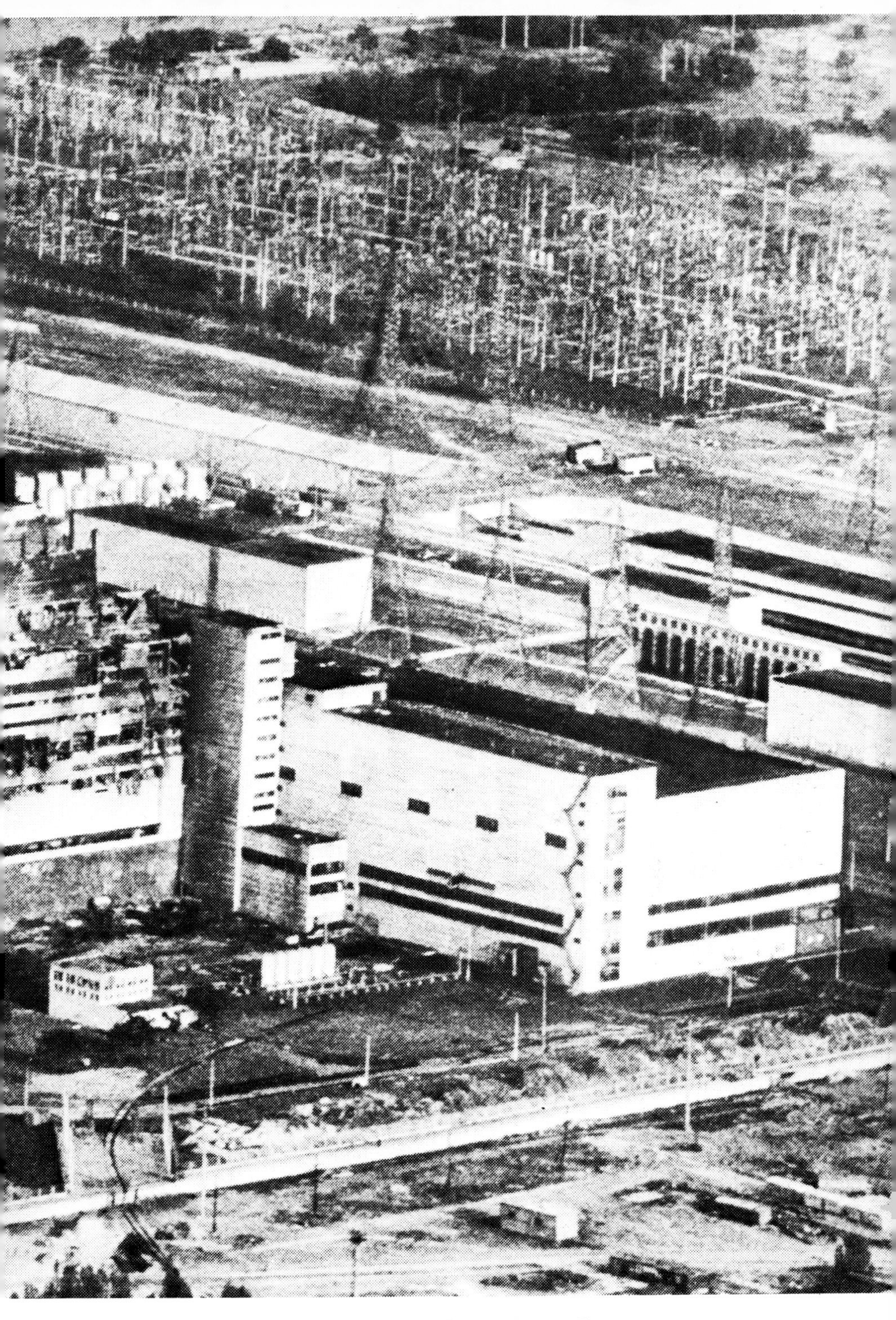

An aerial view of the Chernobyl Atomic Power Plant. The arrow indicates that the accident took place in unit number 4. This photo was taken on May 9, 1986.

General Secretary Gorbachov is warmly greeted by President Reagan upon their meeting at Geneva.

Depicted here is their equally cordial leave-taking of one another after their meeting.

A huge share of the work and responsibility has been taken by the Party, government and economic bodies of the Ukraine and Byelorussia. The operating staff of the Chernobyl nuclear power station are working selflessly and courageously.

So what exactly happened?

As specialists report, the reactor's capacity suddenly increased during a scheduled shut-down of the fourth unit. The considerable emission of steam and subsequent reaction resulted in the formation of hydrogen, which exploded, damaging the reactor and bringing on radioactive emission.

It is still too early to pass a final judgement on the causes of the accident . All aspects of the problem—design, technical and operational—are under the close scrutiny of the Government commission. It goes without saying that when the investigation into the accident is over, all the necessary conclusions will be drawn and measures taken to rule out a repetition of such an occurrence.

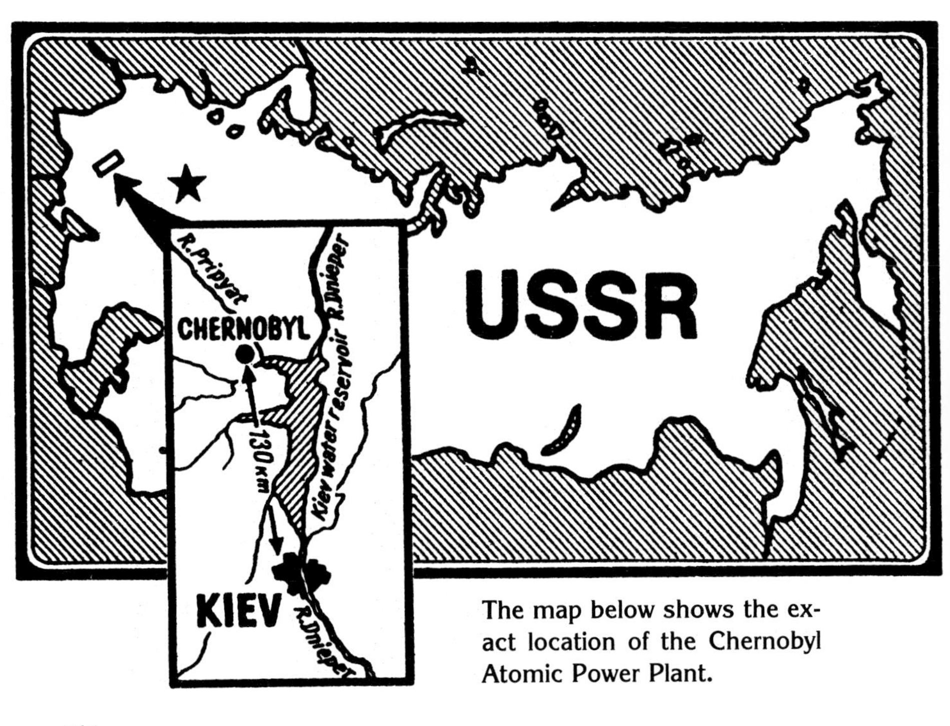

The map below shows the exact location of the Chernobyl Atomic Power Plant.

In Chernobyl's graphite-moderated reactor, a water cooling system is used.

As I have said, it was the first time that we encountered such an emergency when the need arose to quickly curb the dangerous force of the atom that had gone out of control and contain the consequences of the accident.

The seriousness of the situation was obvious. It was necessary to evaluate it immediately and competently. And as soon as we received reliable initial information it was made available to the Soviet people and sent through diplomatic channels to the governments of foreign countries.

On the basis of this information, practical work was launched to correct the situation and limit the grave aftermath of the accident.

In the hazardous situation we considered it our paramount duty, a duty of special importance, to ensure the safety of the population and provide effective assistance to those involved in the accident. The inhabitants of the community near the station were evacuated within a matter of hours and then, when it had become clear that there was a potential threat to the health of people in the adjoining zone, they also were moved to safe areas. All this complex work required utmost speed, organization and precision.

Nevertheless, the measures that were taken failed

Raisa Gorbachov and Nancy Reagan holding hands.

Gorbachov and Mitterand at their joint press conference at the Elysees Palace.

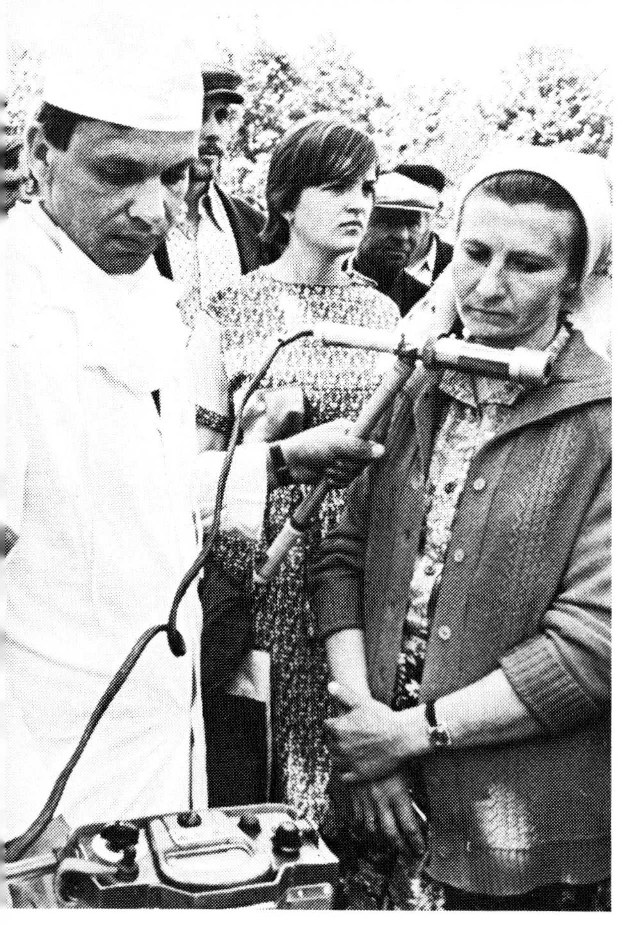

In the Makarovsky district of the Kiev region, a woman who has been evacuated from the Chernobyl area is checked for radiation.

to help many people. Two died at the time of the accident—Vladimir Nikolayevich Shashenok, an adjuster of automatic systems, and Valery Ivanovich Khodemchuk, an operator at the nuclear power plant. As of today 299 people are in hospital with radiation sickness of varying degrees of gravity. Seven of them have died. All possible treatment is being given to the rest. The country's best scientific and medical specialists and specialized clinics in Moscow and other cities are treating them and have at their disposal the most up-to-date methods offered by medicine.

On behalf of the CPSU Central Committee and the Soviet Government, I express profound condolences to the families and relatives of the deceased, to the work collectives, to all who have suffered from this misfortune, who have suffered personal loss. The Soviet Government will take care of the families of those who died or were injured.

The inhabitants of the areas that heartily welcomed the evacuees deserve the highest appreciation. They responded to the misfortune of their neighbours as though it were their own, and in the best traditions of our people displayed consideration, responsiveness and attentiveness.

The CPSU Central Commitee and the Soviet Government are receiving thousands upon thousands of letters and telegrams from Soviet people and also from foreign citizens expressing sympathy and support for the victims. Many Soviet families are prepared to take children into their homes for the summer and are offering material aid. There have been numerous requests to be sent to work in the area of the accident.

These manifestations of humaneness, genuine humanism, high moral standards cannot but move each and every one of us.

Assistance to people, I repeat, remains our top priority.

At the same time vigorous work is under way at the station itself and on the adjacent territory to limit the

Mikhail Gorbachov, during an official visit to East Berlin, talks to a group of young people.

Mikhail Gorbachov talking with workers at the Volga Motor Works in Togliatti, Kuibishev region.

Foreign cameramen watch a dosimetric check in the Makarovsky district of Kiev, which hosted evacuees from Chernobyl.

scale of the accident. In the most difficult conditions it proved possible to extinguish the fire and prevent it from spreading to the other power units.

The staff of the station stopped the three other reactors and put them in a safe state. They are under constant control.

A stiff test has faced and is facing all—firemen, transport and building workers, medics, special chemical protection units, helicopter crews and other detachments of the Ministry of Defense and the Ministry of Internal Affairs.

In these difficult conditions much depended on a correct scientific evaluation of what was happening because without such an evaluation it would have been impossible to work out and apply effective measures to cope with the accident and its aftermath. Prominent scientists from our Academy of Science, leading specialists from the Union Ministries and agencies in the Ukraine and Byelorussia are successfully coping with this task.

I must say that people have acted and are continuing to act heroically, selflessly. I think we will yet have an opportunity to name these courageous people and assess their worthy actions.

I have every reason to state that despite the deep gravity of what happened the damage turned out to be limited owing in a decisive degree to the courage and skill of our people, their loyalty to duty, and the concerted effort to liquidate the aftermath of the accident.

This task, Comrades, is being solved not only in the area of the nuclear power station itself but also in scientific institutes, at many of the country's enterprises which are supplying all essentials to those who are directly involved in the difficult and dangerous effort to deal with the accident.

Thanks to the effective measures taken, we can say today that the worst is over. The most critical consequences have been averted. Of course, there is much left to be done. It is not yet time to rest. Extensive and demanding work still lies ahead. The radiation level in the station zone and in the immediate vicinity still remains dangerous for human health. The top-prior-

During a trip to Berlin, Mikhail Gorbachov addresses a workers' committee at the October 7th factory.

Party Secretary General Gorbachov addressing the Soviet audience about the Chernobyl disaster.

ity task as of today, therefore, is to deal with the consequences of the accident. A large-scale program for the radioactive decontamination of the territory near the power station, of the employee's community, and of buildings and structures has been drawn up and is being implemented. The necessary manpower, material and technical resources have been concentrated for that purpose. In order to prevent radioactive contamination of the water, measures are being taken at the site of the station and on the adjacent territory.

The meteorological service is constantly monitoring the radiation situation on the ground, in the water, and in the atmosphere. They have at their disposal the necessary technical systems and are using specially equipped planes, helicopters and ground monitoring stations.

It is absolutely clear—all these operations will take much time and will require considerable effort. They should be carried out meticulously in a planned and organized manner. The area must be restored to a state that in no way endangers the health and normal life of people.

Mikhail Gorbachov is greeted by residents of Togliatti, in the Kuibyshev region.

In early February of 1986 Gorbachov received the political director, a reporter and the chairman of the foreign section of the French Communist newspaper *Humanite.*

I must not fail to mention one more aspect of this affair, and that is the reaction abroad to what happened at Chernobyl. The world at large, and this should be emphasized, treated with understanding the misfortune that befell us and our actions in that complex situation.

We are profoundly grateful to our friends in Socialist countries who have shown solidarity with the Soviet people at this time of trouble. We are grateful to the political and public figures in other states for their sincere sympathy and support.

We express our kind feelings to foreign scientists and specialists who showed readiness to give assistance in coping with consequences of the accident. I would like to note the participation of the American physicians Robert Gale and Paul Tarasaki in the treatment of the injured and to express gratitude to the business circles of those countries which promptly complied with our request to purchase certain types of equipment, materials and medicine.

A stamp issued to commemorate the 50th anniversary of the establishment of "The Order of Lenin".

A stamp issued in honor of Lenin.

A stamp commemorating the 50th anniversary of the adoption of the first 5-year plan for the development of the national economy.

We appreciate the objective attitude to the events at the Chernobyl nuclear power station on the part of the International Atomic Energy Agency (IAEA) and its Director-General Hans Blix.

In other words, we highly appreciate the sympathy of all those who treated our misfortune and our problems with an open heart.

At the same time it is impossible to pass by without political assessment, the treatment given the event at Chernobyl by the governments, political figures and the mass media in certain NATO countries, especially the USA. They launched an unbridled anti-Soviet campaign. It is difficult to imagine all that has been

A stamp commemorating the "Universal Year of Communication."

Two Soviet stamps issued to commemorate Lenin.

В.И. ЛЕНИН
1985
ПОЧТА СССР 30к
1870-1924

ORBITAL SPACE COMPLEX: COSMOS SPUTNIK-SHIP – SALYUT 7 STATION – SOYUZ TRANSPORT SHIP.

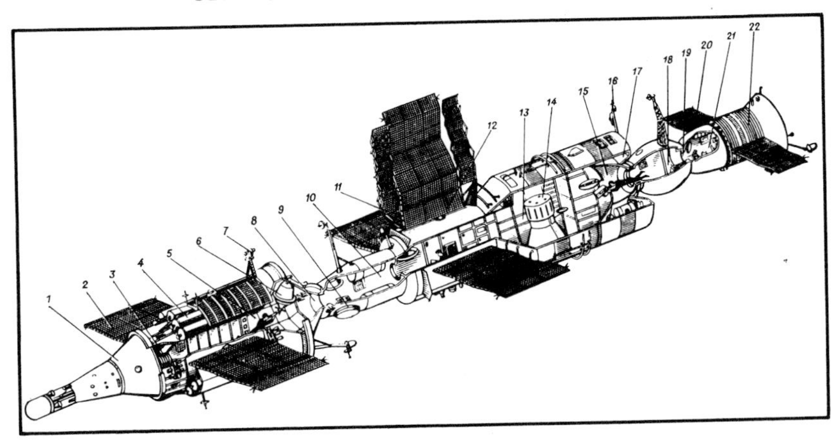

Cosmos sputnik-ship:

1. re-entry vehicle; 2. solar battery; 3. transfer tunnel; 4. fuel tank; 5. operational-service unit; 6. inner transfer hatch; 7. antenna of the radio-technical docking system; 8. docking unit.

Salyut 7 station:

9. hatch for going out to space; 10. transfer compartment; 11. additional solar battery; 12. main solar battery; 13. working compartment; 14. research instruments compartment; 15. transfer module; 16. antenna of radio-technical docking; 17. engine compartment.

Soyuz transport ship:

18. living compartment; 19. hatch for transfer to living compartment; 20. solar battery; 21. descent capsule; 22. instrument compartment.

A diagram of the "Cosmos Sputnik-Ship."

said and written—"thousands of casualties", "mass graves for the dead","Kiev desolate", "the land of the Ukraine poisoned", and so on and so forth.

Generally speaking, we faced a veritable mountain of lies—most dishonest and malicous lies. It is unpleasant to recall all this, but it must be done. The international community must know what we had to face. This must be done to find the answer to the question: what, in actual fact, was behind that highly immoral campaign?

Its organizers, to be sure, were interested neither in the truth about the accident nor in the fate of the people at Chernobyl, in the Ukraine, in Byelorussia, in any other place, any other country. They needed a pretext for defaming the Soviet Union (its foreign policy), for lessening the impact of Soviet proposals regarding the termination of nuclear tests and the elimination of nuclear weapons, and at the same time, for dampening the growing criticism of US conduct on the international scene and of its militaristic course.

Bluntly speaking, certain Western politicians were after very definite results. They were out to blast the

During a visit to East Berlin, Mikhail Gorbachov meets with East German leader Eric Honneker.

possibilities for smoothing out international relations, to sow new seeds of mistrust and suspicion toward the socialist countries.

All this made itself clearly felt during the meeting of the leaders of "the Seven" held not long ago in Tokyo. What did they tell the world, what dangers did they warn mankind of? Of Libya, groundlessly accused of terrorism, and also of the Soviet Union which, it turns out, failed to provide them with "full" information about the accident at Chernobyl. And not a word about the most important thing—how to stop the arms race, how to rid the world of the nuclear threat. Not a word in reply to the Soviet initiatives, to our definite proposals for ending nuclear tests, ridding mankind of nuclear and chemical weapons and reducing conventional arms.

How should all this be interpreted? One gets the impression that the leaders of the capitalist powers who gathered in Tokyo wanted to use the Chernobyl accident as a pretext for distracting the attention of the world public from all those problems that make them uncomfortable, but are so real and important for the whole world.

A stamp reproduction of K. Filator's picture *Lenin at the Red Square.*

President Reagan replies while General Secretary Gorbachov listens attentively. The two heads of state are two of the most powerful men in the world.

THE MIR ORBITAL RESEARCH STATION.
BASE UNIT.

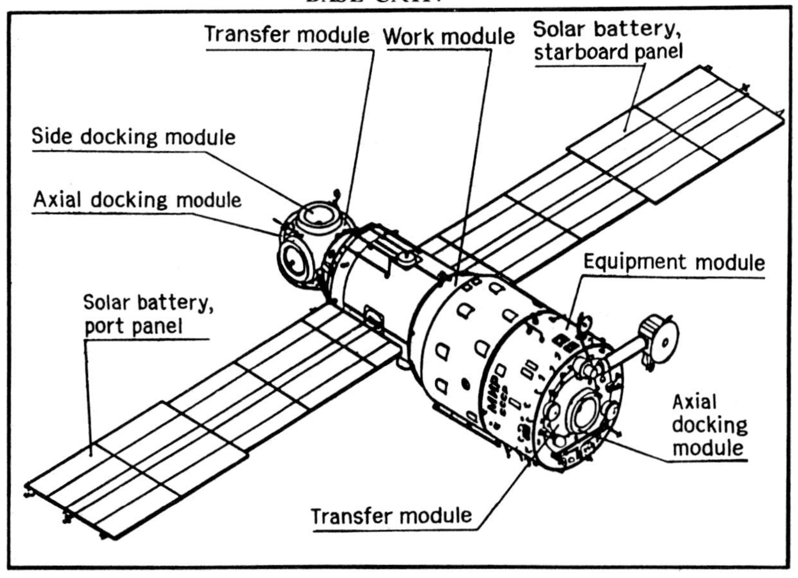

A diagram of the "Mir Orbital Research Station."

The reaction to the accident at the Chernobyl station has become a kind of a test of political morality. Once again two different approaches, two different lines of conduct were revealed for everyone to see.

The ruling circles of the USA and their most zealous allies—especially West Germany—regarded the occurrence as just another possibility to put up additional obstacles to the development and deepening of the East-West dialogue, which is progressing slowly as it is, and to justify the nuclear arms race. Moreover, an attempt has been made to prove to the world that talks and hence agreements with the USSR are impossible, and thus to give a green light to further military preparations.

Our attitude to this tragedy is completely different. We realize that it is another signal of alarm, another grim warning that the nuclear era calls for new political thinking and a new policy.

This has strengthened still more our conviction that the foreign policy course established by the 27th CPSU Congress is correct and that our proposals for the complete elimination of nuclear weapons, the ending of nuclear explosions, and the creation of an all-embracing system of international security meet those inexorably stringent demands which the nuclear age makes of the political leadership of all countries.

As to the "lack" of information, over which a special campaign, a political campaign, has been launched, it is an invention. The following confirms this. It took the US authorities ten days to inform their own Congress and months to inform the world community about the tragedy that took place at Three Mile Island atomic power station in 1979.

I have already said how we acted.

All this enables one to judge who approaches in what way the matter of informing their own people and foreign countries.

A stamp commemorating the achievements of Lenin.

Mikhail Gorbachov is greeted by children in Togliatti, Kuibyshev region.

But this is not the main thing. We hold that the accident at Chernobyl, just like the accidents at US, British and other atomic power stations poses very serious problems to all states, problems which require a responsible attitude.

Over 370 atomic reactors are now functioning in different countries. This is reality. The future of the world economy can hardly be imagined without the development of atomic energy. Altogether 40 reactors with an aggregate capacity of over 28 million kilowatts are now operating in our country. Mankind derives considerable benefit from the atom when it is used for peaceful purposes.

But it stands to reason that we are all obliged to act with still greater caution, to direct science and technology at ensuring the safe harnessing of the great and formidable nuclear power.

The indisputable lesson Chernobyl gave us is that in conditions of the further development of the scientific and technical revolution the questions of reliability and safety of equipment, the questions of discipline, order and organization take on paramount importance. The most stringent demands everywhere and in everything are needed.

Further, we deem it necessary to request a serious deepening of cooperation within the framework of the International Atomic Energy Agency (IAEA). What could be done in this respect?

First, creating an international regime of safe development of nuclear power on the basis of close cooperation between all nations dealing with nuclear power engineering. A system of early warning and supply of information in the event of accidents or malfunctions at nuclear power stations, specifically when this is accompanied by radioactive emission, should be established under such a regime. Likewise it is necessary to adjust an international mechanism, both on a bilateral and multilateral basis, for the speediest rendering of mutual assistance when dangerous situations emerge.

Second, for the discussion of the entire range of matters it would be justifiable to convene a highly au-

A stamp commemorating the 109th anniversary of Lenin's birth.

thoritative special international conference in Vienna under IAEA auspices.

Third, in view of the fact that the IAEA was founded back in 1957 and that its resources and staff are not in keeping with the level of the development of present-day nuclear power engineering, it would be expedient to enhance the role and possibilities of that unique international organization. The Soviet Union is ready for this.

Fourth, it is our conviction that the United Nations Organisation and its specialised agencies, such as the World Health Organisation (WHO) and the United Nations Environmental Programme (UNEP), should be more actively involved in the effort to ensure safe development of peaceful nuclear activity.

Considering all this, it should not be forgotten that in our world, where everything is interdependent, there exist, alongside problems of atoms for peace, problems of atoms for war. This is the main thing now. The accident at Chernobyl showed once again what an abyss will open up if nuclear war strikes mankind. For nuclear stockpiles are fraught with thousands upon thousands of disasters far more horrible than the Chernobyl one.

In conditions of increased attention to nuclear matters, the Soviet government, having considered all circumstances connected with the security of its people and all of humanity, has decided to extend its unilateral moratorium on nuclear tests till August 6 of this year, that is till the date on which more than 40 years ago the first atomic bomb was dropped on the Japanese city of Hiroshima, as a result of which hundreds of thousands of people perished.

We again urge the United States to consider with utmost responsibility the degree of danger looming over mankind, to heed the opinion of the world community. Let those who lead the United States show their concern for the life and health of people by their deeds.

I confirm my proposal to President Reagan to meet without delay in the capital of any European state that will be prepared to accept us or, say, in Hiroshima and to agree on a ban on nuclear testing.

The nuclear age forcefully demands a new approach to international relations, the pooling of efforts of states with different social systems for the sake of ending the disastrous arms race and radically improving the world political climate. Broad horizons will then be cleared for fruitful cooperation between all countries and peoples, and all men on earth will gain from that.

A mural
which depicts Moscow as a booming metropolis and exhorts citizens to achieve perfect Communism.

To Visitors of Soviet Pavilion At Expo-86 World Exhibition In Vancouver

I wholeheartedly greet the visitors of the Soviet pavilion at the EXPO-86 World Exhibition in Vancouver.

The Soviet Union highly appraised the initiative of the government of Canada on organising this Exhibition and willingly took part in it because our country, like Canada, is particularly interested in the development of transport and communication because of the vastness of its territory.

The USSR's pavilion at the Exhibition will give its visitors an idea of the great efforts the Soviet people, engaged in peaceful constructive work, make to develop these sectors of the national economy. In the past few years the unique Baikal-Amur trunk railway has been built in our country in difficult natural conditions, a number of Siberia-Western Europe pipelines have been built, the transportation of cargoes by the Northern Sea Route developed intensively with the use of up-to-date nuclear-powered ice-breakers, the automobile fleet has been considerably built up, and many new air routes, including some to the Far North areas, have been put into service. An integrated automated communication network was further developed on the basis of the advances of science and technology. All this made for the further social and economic progress of the more than 100 nations, big and small, who live in our country, for the extension of their intercourse, and for the strengthening of friendship. The plans provide for large-scale measures to develop transport lines and communication in the Soviet Union also in the period up to the year 2000.

As is known, some countries represented at the EXPO-86, among them Canada, have made great advances in the sphere of transport and communication. In my view, the exchange of experiences and achievements among the participants in the Exhibition will be fruitful and will serve to promote cooperation and confidence among nations.

The Soviet Union consistently stands for widest trade, economic, scientific, technological and cultural cooperation with all states. This policy-line has found its clear expression in the resolutions adopted at the 27th Congress of the Communist Party of the Soviet Union.

Peace and cooperation are the prime aim of the Soviet foreign policy. The Soviet proposals, aimed at cessation of the arms race and nuclear tests, at elimination of the nuclear threat and at complete disarmament, serve to attain this aim. This is the essence of the Soviet foreign-policy initiatives advanced by General Secretary of the CPSU Central Committee Mikhail Gorbachov on January 15, 1986.

The USSR's pavilion at the Exhibition will certainly help its visitors to feel more deeply the vital interest of the Soviet people in preserving peace, their peaceability and the humanitarian orientation of their constructive work both in outer space and on the Earth.

The Soviet Union attaches great importance to the traditional relations with Canada, our esteemed Northern neighbour, and is willing to develop and refine these relations.

Expressing the feelings of the Soviet people, I convey to the Canadian people the wishes of success and prosperity.

Endpapers:
President Reagan listens attentively as Party General Secretary Gorbachov makes an address at the Geneva summit meeting in 1985.